The Adventures of Hiram Holliday: The Scripts

The Adventures of Hiram Holliday: The Scripts

Volume One

Edited by Ian Dickerson

BearManor Media
2023

The Adventures of Hiram Holliday: The Scripts
Volume One

© *2023 Ian Dickerson*

All rights reserved.

Published in the United States of America by:

BearManor Media

4700 Millenia Blvd.
Suite 175 PMB 90497
Orlando, FL 32839

bearmanormedia.com

Printed in the United States.

Typesetting and layout by PKJ Passion Global

ISBN—979-8-88771-161-4

This one's for Helen and Ted, with love.

Table of Contents

Introduction

The half hour sitcom *The Adventures of Hiram Holliday* ran for less than six months on NBC from the tail end of 1956 through to early the following year, yet it remains fondly in the memories of a generation despite its short life.

Expectations for the show had been high; it was based on a handful of books by renowned author Paul Gallico and the star, Wally Cox himself, was just coming off a three-year run as the very popular *Mister Peepers* for the same network. On top of that, the show was produced, directed and largely written by Philip Rapp, who'd had a stellar career in radio as the creator of Baby Snooks and *The Bickersons* and had recently been writing for the CBS show *Topper*.

Encouraged by that the network scheduled the show against *Walt Disney's Disneyland*—Disney's first TV show which had recently started running on ABC and garnered sizeable ratings—and *The Arthur Godfrey Show*—an hour-long variety show hosted by the popular entertainer. Poor old Hiram didn't stand a chance. The show was yanked off the network before every episode had aired, with the sponsor willing to take a sizeable financial hit rather than let the show struggle onwards.

The story behind what happened has been documented elsewhere but what's left behind, whether on screen or in print, are a number of fascinating stories. So we figured it's time you got to read some of them…

The Adventure of the Lapidary Wheel

This was the second script to be commissioned and, indeed, the second episode to air. NBC aired it on 10 October 1956 whilst the BBC aired it on 3 August 1960 and again on 29 January the following year. It was written, produced and directed by the show's creator, Philip Rapp. Early on Rapp discovered that Wally Cox was a rock collector in real life so when Hiram is busy polishing squares of rose quartz for a chessboard, he was using Cox's own lapidary wheel. The cast in this episode included John Abbott as the Headmaster, Pamela Light as Ada, John Colicos as Ernest and John Alderson as the Policeman.

FADE IN:

EXT. OCEAN LINER-DAY-FULL SHOT (STOCK)

A liner of the luxury class is ploughing through the ocean.

DISSOLVE:

EXT. DECK-DAY-MED. SHOT

The ship's CAPTAIN and the MATE are at the rail, peering down to the water below. Their attitude is tense and strained. Behind them stands a small knot of passengers.

CAPTAIN

It was madness to let him go down there... madness! Even if the ship is hopelessly disabled!

MATE

He's been submerged for fourteen minutes, Captain.

The Captain takes a quick look at his watch.

CAPTAIN

No man can stay under the North Atlantic that long and come up alive!

MATE

He's coming up!

The Captain looks down, staring.

CAPTAIN

He is coming up! Incredible!

(calls off)

Ready the decompression chamber.

CAMERA PULLS BACK as a dripping figure in a frogman's outfit climbs up a Jacob's ladder and over the rail. He is carrying a pipe wrench in his hand.

CAPTAIN

(continuing, anxiously)

Are you all right? Are you all right?

CAMERA MOVES IN again as the figure pulls off his face mask and we see it is HIRAM HOLLIDAY.

HIRAM

It was only the rubber and I straightened it. We must have hit a whale.

He hands the wrench to the engineer. We can see the grip is bent like a boomerang.

CAPTAIN

Sir, how can myself, every man, woman, and child on board this ship express what we owe to you?

HIRAM

The pleasure was all mine. I found a rare Lepas fascicularis clinging to the hull.

CAPTAIN

(quizzically)

Lepas?

HIRAM

Lepas fascicularis -- a goose barnacle.

He holds up the barnacle, as the Captain and Engineer stare.

HIRAM

(continuing, moving off)

I collect barnacles.

He removes the small oxygen tank from his back with the aid of the mate. As he does so he indicates a valve.

HIRAM

(continuing)

Incidentally, you'd better have that fixed. I couldn't get the oxygen valve open.

He flaps off with his swim fins as the Captain and Mate stare after him and then at one another. The little group of passengers is stunned.

GIRL

(to Captain)

Who is that man, Captain?

CAPTAIN

That man is the last of the romantic heroes, his name is Hiram Holliday.

GIRL

(astonished)

That!

The CAMERA PANS OFF to Joel who is leaning over the rail alone. He is looking in the direction of the group.

SMITH

Yes, that.

(to CAMERA)

That's Hiram Holliday and I'm Joel Smith, reporter with the New York Chronicle. Two weeks ago, Hiram's expert proof reading save the paper from a million dollar libel suit and won him a bonus and a trip around the world. The story I'm working on?

(raises pad)

The Adventures of Hiram Holliday. In six hours we will be in London.

(smiles)

I think Madame Tussaud better start heating up her wax.

FADE OUT:

FADE IN:

MONTAGE-DAY-(STOCK)

This is a MONTAGE of familiar London landmarks that ESTAB-LISHED the city. The final SHOT is that of Maiden Lane. SUPER-IMPOSED is the word for "LONDON".

INT. JEWEL MERCHANT'S STORE-DAY-FULL SHOT

The shop has an air and tradition of comfortable affluence. Hiram, his ever-present umbrella in hand, is looking around, and is approached by a SALESMAN who looks more like a banker. There is one other customer in the shop; a dignified gentleman who is examining a stone on display. He is dressed almost like a clergyman, but is in fact wearing the everyday costume of a Headmaster of a Scottish Boys' School. The HEADMASTER is engrossed in a gem which reposes on black velvet in a glass case.

SALESMAN

(to Hiram)

Good afternoon?

HIRAM

I would like to look at lapidary wheels.

SALESMAN

Lapidary wheels?

HIRAM

Preferably one with a scavenger pump.

The salesman, with admirable British restraint, raises one eyebrow just a fraction.

SALESMAN

Scavenger pump.

HIRAM

Yes.

SALESMAN

I believe that I shall have to consult with our Mr. Higginbotham.

HIRAM

Thank you.

The salesman goes off to the back of the shop. Hiram looks around and catches the eye of the Headmaster who smiles.

HEADMASTER

(Scottish)

I heard you ask for a lapidary wheel. You're a gem cutter?

HIRAM

Not exactly, I'm making a chess board with stones.

HEADMASTER

Here's one that would fit nicely in your board.

He indicates the stone on display. Hiram walks over to look at it and the headmaster points.

CLOSE SHOT-LARGE DIAMOND

HEADMASTER'S VOICE

(continuing)

The Sorrow of Shahbandar. Two hundred and fifty-two carats.

TWO SHOT- HIRAM AND HEADMASTER

HIRAM

(the epee point)

Ooh.

HEADMASTER

Perhaps the world's most perfect first quality diamond. I come to look everyday but not tomorrow.

                    HIRAM

Really?

                  HEADMASTER

It's going home to India.

                    HIRAM

               (with sympathy)

I don't suppose they'd let you buy it.

                  HEADMASTER

The Headmaster of a Scottish school may only gaze at the
Shahbandar.

CLOSE TWO SHOT-P.O.V. OF THE DIAMOND

Both Hiram and the Headmaster gaze in the direction of the stone.
                                        DISSOLVE:

INT. HOTEL ROOM-DAY-FULL SHOT

Hiram is bent over his lapidary wheel as Joel enters.

                    SMITH

What on earth is that?

Hiram looks up.

                    HIRAM

Hi, Joel.

                  (proudly)

It's my lapidary wheel complete with scavenger pump.

SMITH

Make it yourself?

HIRAM

As a guest in the country, I didn't think that would be right. Competing with the English worker.

SMITH

Oh, haven't you unpacked yet Hiram?

He points to Hiram's bag which is closed.

HIRAM

I'm taking a little run up to Scotland tonight.

SMITH

Scotland???

HIRAM

Pittenweem Glenn that is near Firth of Forth. They have some quite unusual igneous rocks.

SMITH

You're going all the way to Scotland to pick up rocks?

HIRAM

For my chessboard. It's the chance of a lifetime.

SMITH

Hiram...

HIRAM

Oh, you don't have to come, Joel. Although it sounds quite interesting.

Joel sinks down into a chair wearily.

SMITH

I wouldn't miss it for the world. Igneous rocks...Did you say Firth of Forth?

HIRAM

Firth of Forth.

SMITH

Then I'd better take along a fifth.

As Hiram gives him a puzzled look.

DISSOLVE:

EXT. TRAIN-NIGHT-FULL SHOT (STOCK)

The train is moving slowly, just picking up speed.

INT. TRAIN-MED. SHOT

Hiram and Joel with their bags are moving along the corridor looking for an empty compartment. Joel puts down his bag.

SMITH

Hiram you find a compartment. I want to get to the diner before it gets crowded.

HIRAM

(clutching bag and umbrella)

You go ahead, Joel. I'm not hungry yet.

Joel moves off the other way leaving his bag and Hiram moves on along the corridor, CAMERA MOVING WITH HIM. After passing one more compartment he sees one occupied by only one passenger, opens the door and goes in.

INT. COMPARTMENT-MED. SHOT

The shades are drawn almost to the bottom of the windows. A turbaned HINDU is sitting in one of the seats as Hiram enters. He is reading a book written in Hindustani.

HIRAM

I hope I'm not intruding?

The Hindu inclines his head slightly and continues reading.

HIRAM

(continuing)

Thank you.

He stows away his baggage. The only baggage of the Hindu is a woven basket in the corner of the compartment.

HIRAM

(continuing)

I have to get my friend's bag, excuse me.

He leaves as the Hindu inclines his head again and returns to his book.

INT. CORRIDOR-MED. SHOT

Hiram works his way down the narrow corridor, swaying with the movement of the train, and picks up Joel's bag. As he turns, he runs smack into a London BOBBY coming the other way. The uniformed Bobby carries a bag and several magazines. In trying to extricate himself from the tangle that results, Hiram yanks hard at Joel's bag, and it flies open. A bottle of scotch rolls out.

BOBBY

(looks at the bottle then at Hiram, grimly)

Can't travel about without your neat and frisky, eh?

HIRAM

(recovers bottle)

I know that is Australian rhyming slang for whisky.

He favors the Bobby with a hopeful smile.

BOBBY

(unsmiling)

Is it now?

HIRAM

(holding up the bottle)

Anyway, this isn't mine, Constable. It belongs to my companion. But I'm sure that under the circumstances he'd want me to offer you a drink.

He offers the Bobby the bottle.

BOBBY

No, thank you. I'm on duty.

With that he pushes past Hiram and exits the scene. Hiram replaces the bottle in the bag, is about to start back to his compartment, and then does a big take at the Bobby's retort. With a shrug he starts back to his compartment and enters.

INT. COMPARTMENT-MED. SHOT

The Hindu is sitting in the same position, staring straight ahead as Hiram enters. The book is in his lap held lightly in his hands.

HIRAM

Back again.

He starts stowing away Joel's bag and talking over his shoulder to the Hindu.

HIRAM
(continuing)

My friend's in the dining car.

He surveys the position of the two bags and then makes a minor readjustment.

HIRAM
(continuing)

Do you know what time we get to Prestwick?

There is no response and after a while he turns to the Hindu speaking as he turns.

HIRAM
(continuing)

Say! It just occurred to me would you rather converse in Hindustani?

(in Hindustani)

Can you please tell me what time we...

CLOSE SHOT-THE HINDU

As the train rounds a curve, he rolls from his sitting position and pitches forward on the floor, quite dead, with a large knife in his back. The train WHISTLES.

TWO SHOT -- HIRAM AND THE HINDU

HIRAM
(continuing looking down)

Well now.

FULL SHOT-COMPARTMENT

After a moment's deliberation, Hiram goes to the door having to step over the body in passing. He opens the door and goes out into the corridor.

INT. CORRIDOR-MED. SHOT

Hiram works his way forward toward the CAMERA again MOVING WITH HIM as he goes.

INT. DINING CAR-FULL SHOT

Joel Smith is just beginning to eat as Hiram comes forward through the dining car.

SMITH

Hiram! Ready to eat?

HIRAM

(not pausing)

I don't think I'm hungry yet.

He goes off, CAMERA STAYING with Joel, who looks after Hiram, slightly puzzled as to where he is going.

INT. CORRIDOR-MED. SHOT

Hiram comes into the picture, we see through the door of the compartment the Bobby with whom Hiram has tangled just previously. He is making himself at home in the empty compartment, taking off his shoes with an air of supreme relief and satisfaction.

INT. COMPARTMENT-MED. SHOT

Hiram enters the compartment. The Bobby looks up and sees who it is expressing no joy at the meeting.

BOBBY

What do you want?

HIRAM

I suppose I wish to report a crime.

BOBBY

(dismissing him)

How many times do I have to tell you? I'm off duty!

He picks up a paper and starts to read.

HIRAM

Oh.

(slight pause)

Could you recommend anyone else?

BOBBY

(putting his paper down)

What's this horrible crime?

HIRAM

You see, when I first went into my compartment, there was a Hindu gentleman there. No, Hindu is not the correct term pertaining to religion rather than...

BOBBY

Was he there or wasn't he there??

HIRAM

He was, yes. He nodded to me twice, I believe. Then I left for a moment; that's when I met you, if you remember...

BOBBY

I remember.

HIRAM

...and on my return, I asked the gentleman if he would care to converse in Hindustani. He made no response, being dead.

BOBBY

(not impressed)

Killed by shock.

HIRAM

(weighing this)

I think not. There was a large knife in his back.

BOBBY

And where is this dead Indoo, with a knife in his back?

HIRAM

In my compartment.

He points. The Bobby starts to pull on his shoes wearily.

BOBBY

All right, let's have a look at him.

HIRAM

(gratefully)

I'd really feel much better about it.

Hiram leads the way out of the compartment into the corridor.

INT. CORRIDOR-MEN. SHOT

They work their way back to the dining car, CAMERA MOVING WITH THEM.

INT. DINING CAR-FULL SHOT

Joel is eating heartily, his back to Hiram. Hiram comes into the picture. Hiram speaks to him without stopping.

HIRAM

Hi, Joel.

Joel sees the Bobby following Hiram, and does a "What is he up to now?" take.

INT. CORRIDOR-MED. SHOT

Hiram and the Bobby work their way to Hiram's compartment, the CAMERA MOVING IN WITH THEM.

HIRAM

Here it is.

The Bobby gives him a look.

                    BOBBY

After you.

Hiram opens the compartment door.

INT. COMPARTMENT-MED. SHOT

CAMERA IS SHOOTING toward door as Hiram enters, speaking over his shoulder to the Bobby.

                    HIRAM

You'll have to step over him as you come in.

The Bobby enters and stares. Hiram has stepped over nothing but air. The compartment is empty.

                    BOBBY

You forgot to tell me it was an invisible 'Indoo.

Hiram looks down.

                    HIRAM

He was right here.

He puts a finger to his lips and is thinking it over.

                    BOBBY

Maybe he was one of the small-size ones. 'Iding under a tea-cup somewhere.

                    HIRAM

No, he was quite large. With a large turban.

                (points to basket)

That's his luggage.

BOBBY

Naturally tell me, do you always see dead 'Indoos when you've had one too many?

HIRAM

I make it a rule never to indulge.

BOBBY
(sarcastically)

That's right, it was your companion's bottle.

(turns to go)

If your 'Indoo comes back again have him show you the Indian Rope trick.

He leaves and Hiram sits down. He stares at the woven basket in the corner.

CLOSE SHOT-BASKET

MED. SHOT-COMPARTMENT

Hiram rises and goes over to the basket. After looking at it a moment he lifts the lid.

CLOSE SHOT-BASKET

As the lid is raised a large king cobra sways up out of the basket with its hood extended.

MED. SHOT-COMPARTMENT

With a quick move Hiram bangs the lid of the basket down again and closes the loose hasp.

CLOSE SHOT-HIRAM

He straightens up thinking it is over then gives a small shrug and turns to leave the compartment.

INT. CORRIDOR-MED. SHOT

Hiram works his way forward, CAMERA MOVING WITH HIM again, as he makes his way past other passengers in the narrow corridor.

INT. DINING ROOM-FULL SHOT

Joel Smith is occupied with his food and does not see Hiram coming until he is almost up to him.

> HIRAM

Hello, Joel.

As Hiram goes by without stopping, Joel swivels around to stare after him.

INT. COMPARTMENT-MED. SHOT

The Bobby is just settled in his compartment, taking a sandwich out of a sack. He looks up as Hiram appears at the door and knocks. After seeing who it is, he decides to ignore him, and is just about to bite into his sandwich as Hiram opens the door.

> HIRAM

Guess what?

> BOBBY

> (matter of fact)

The 'Indoo came back.

> HIRAM

As a matter of fact, no.

BOBBY

Good.

HIRAM

But there is something else in my compartment.

BOBBY

A cobra.

HIRAM

How did you know?

BOBBY

Most of them see cobras first, then dead 'Indoos.

HIRAM

That's very interesting.

BOBBY

Happens every day.

HIRAM

I thought it was most unusual.

BOBBY

Not in my line.

HIRAM

Oh.

The Bobby, considering the conversation at an end, is about to bite into his sandwich. He sees that Hiram is still standing.

> BOBBY

Well?

> HIRAM

What shall I do with the cobra?

> BOBBY

> (exploding)

Knot him up and use him for a blinking bow tie!

> HIRAM

Don't let my outward show of calm deceive you. Actually I'm in a state of shock as you may plainly detect from the extrusion of the papillae of my skin, a condition known as cutis anserina or goose flesh.

The Bobby gives up and rises.

> BOBBY

Here we go again. Let's take a look at your ruddy cobra.

> HIRAM

You won't regret it. He's quite a beautiful specimen.

He goes out of the door with the Bobby following.

INT. CORRIDOR-MED. SHOT

The two start back toward Hiram's compartment.

INT. DINING CAR-FULL SHOT

Joel Smith is eating again as Hiram comes into the picture, passing him without stopping, and the Bobby is following close behind.

HIRAM

Hi, Joel.

Joel does another amazed take at the procession.

INT. CORRIDOR-MED. SHOT

Hiram and the Bobby arrive at the door of Hiram's compartment.
Hiram opens the door.

INT. COMPARTMENT-MED. SHOT

Hiram comes in gesturing to the basket.

HIRAM

He's in that basket.

BOBBY

In the basket, eh? He's in a good frame of mind?

HIRAM

I think I would advise caution. The Naja hannah, or Indian
cobra can cause death within a matter of minutes.

BOBBY

Maybe the snake stabbed the 'Indoo.

Hiram ignores this, picking up his umbrella. He approaches the
basket and extends his umbrella tip toward it and gingerly starts to
raise the lid.

CLOSE TWO SHOT-HIRAM AND THE BOBBY

They are peering at the basket. The tension mounts as Hiram raises
the lid higher.

CLOSE SHOT-BASKET

The lid is being raised all the way but nothing emerges.

MED. SHOT-COMPARTMENT

Hiram and the Bobby are looking at the empty basket.

HIRAM

Isn't that strange. The cobra's not there!

BOBBY

I never would have guessed it.

He walks to the door without a word and goes out; reappearing almost immediately.

BOBBY
(continuing)

If I hear any more of your hanky-panky about cobras and 'Indoos, off the train you go -- off-duty or no off duty!

Hiram looks after him then picks up the basket and turns it upside down.

CLOSE SHOT-HIRAM

He gives a small shrug.

INT. CORRIDOR-ANOTHER ANGLE

As the Bobby stamps down the corridor and out of the picture, a man who has been watching him disappear pulls his head back into his compartment. We see it is the Headmaster.

INT. HEADMASTER'S COMPARTMENT-MED. SHOT

The Headmaster turns from the door back into his compartment. His two traveling companions are a tall and athletic Englishman who is well-dressed but pretty much of a tough and a sultry-look-ing young Englishwomen, dressed in a tight skirt and sweater. The young tough speaks.

ERNIE

What did the Bobby want?

HEADMASTER

I'm not concerned with what he wanted. He knows nothing. I'm concerned with how you two missed the Shahbandar! Where is the gem???

ADA

But we searched him again, Headmaster. Before we threw the body off the train.

The Headmaster turns to her caustically.

HEADMASTER

Thank you, my dear. I would have forgotten that.

(resumes)

Well, I will tell you where the gem is. A lone hand playing a most dangerous game has out-played the three of us.

ADA

Who?

HEADMASTER

The American.

ERNIE
(incredulous)

Him?

HEADMASTER

Yes.

ADA

Let me take care of him.

HEADMASTER

No. When he leaves his compartment I want both of you to turn it inside out. Inside and out.

ERNIE

What if he has it on him?

HEADMASTER

(slowly)

Then, Ernest, more work for your knife.

Cautiously, the Headmaster goes to the door of the compartment and looks out.

INT. CORRIDOR-SAME ANGLE AS PREVIOUS

Hiram emerges from the door of his compartment and walks down the corridor. Over his shoulder, we can see the Headmaster watching him, as we–

FADE OUT

END OF ACT ONE

ACT TWO

FADE IN:

MED. SHOT-CORRIDOR

Hiram is coming down the narrow corridor toward his compartment. He suddenly comes face to face with Ada and as the train lurches around a bend she is in his arms.

                    ADA

          (casually remaining in his arms)

   Do you have a match?

She puts a cigarette in her mouth.

                    HIRAM

          (still holding her bent over)

   Not a match, no. But since I never travel without the necessary equipment for creating a fire by friction...

He gestures toward his compartment.

                    ADA

   I'd have to go into your compartment? Alone?

                    HIRAM

          (releasing her)

   You wait here and I will take the cigarette.

She moves around him slowly and he turns with her so that his back is now toward his compartment door.

ADA

I do not know if I should trust you or myself.

HIRAM

(with a slight laugh)

Well, you know yourself better than I do.

Over his speech the door to his compartment opens and Ernie slips out, giving Ada the high sign. He then goes swiftly toward his own compartment and enters.

ADA

Perhaps some other time.

HIRAM

Gladly.

She moves away up the corridor and Hiram turns to his compartment, just a few steps away and enters the door.

CLOSE SHOT-HIRAM

He reacts as he enters the door of his compartment.

FULL SHOT-COMPARTMENT-HIRAM'S POV

The compartment has been thoroughly ransacked. The bags are lying open, with clothes and other belongings strewn over the floor.

MED. SHOT-COMPARTMENT

Hiram enters looking around. He then bends over to straighten things up. He is stuffing clothes back into the suitcases when the Headmaster comes in the door behind him and stands at the door for a moment looking around. At the back of the Headmaster are Ernie and Ada.

HEADMASTER

You keep an untidy house, sir.

Hiram straightens up, looking around.

HIRAM

Oh, how do you do? Just throw some shirts on the floor and sit down.

He gestures toward the littered seats.

HEADMASTER

No, thank you. Your remember Maiden Lane?

HIRAM

Yes, you admired the Sorrow of Shahbandar.

HEADMASTER

The Sorrow of Shahbandar. Allow me to present my secretary and the Greek instructor at my school.

The Headmaster indicates first Ada and then Ernie.

HIRAM

Very nice to meet you. Hiram Holliday.

HEADMASTER

We are delighted, Mr. Holliday.

With the cane that he is carrying, he fastidiously moves some socks off a seat and sits down.

HEADMASTER
(continuing)

I believe I will sit down.

Ada and Ernie continue to stand by the door.

> HEADMASTER
> (continuing)

What is the purpose of your trip to Scotland, Mr. Holliday?

> HIRAM

I intend to pick up some rocks.

> HEADMASTER

Indeed, a collector.

> HIRAM

Just in an amateur sort of way.

> HEADMASTER

I doubt that extremely. It was not the mark of an amateur to know that the Shahbandar would be on this train.

> HIRAM

Really?

> HEADMASTER

To know that it would be on the flight to India and leaving from Prestwick.

> ERNIE
> (impatiently)

Let's get on with it!

> HEADMASTER
> (ignoring him)

I admire your approach, Mr. Holliday. You watched us and when we bungled, you stepped in. By the way, you have the stone on you?

HIRAM

How much are you prepared to pay?

HEADMASTER

Just what we paid the Hindu.

(rising)

A fair wage.

HIRAM

There's just one thing. Tradition says that the Sorrow of Shahbander has a guardian whose eyes never close.

ERNIE

His eyes were closed right enough when we chucked him off the train.

HIRAM

(to the Headmaster)

You know the legend?

HEADMASTER

Hindu superstition. The stone please, Ernie.

Ernie suddenly has a knife in his hand and he advances on Hiram.

ADA

(suddenly)

Look!!

She points to the basket in the corner in which the lid has been left open.

CLOSE SHOT-BASKET

The cobra is swaying up out of the basket.

FULL SHOT-COMPARTMENT

Ernie, the Headmaster, and the girl all shrink back from the cobra.

ERNIE

Keep him off me!

HIRAM

The guardian of the gem is Kala Nag.

ADA

It's a cobra and he's deadly!

HIRAM

Only if you show fear.

HEADMASTER

Kala Nag...I never believed...

(suddenly, to Hiram)

He's going to strike -- do something!

HIRAM

Do you happen to have a flute with you?

HEADMASTER

No!!!

HIRAM

I suppose I shall have to improvise.

He takes a comb out of his pocket and picks up some paper from the belongings strewn around the floor.

ADA

What are you going to do?

HIRAM

It is said that music has a certain therapeutic value in soothing the hamadryad or king cobra.

He puts the paper over the comb and blows a note for pitch.

CLOSE SHOT-BASKET

The cobra has come higher out of the basket and seems about to strike.

HEADMASTER'S VOICE

Quick, Holliday! Quick!!

FULL SHOT-COMPARTMENT

Hiram turns to the Headmaster.

HIRAM

Do you have a favorite tune?

HEADMASTER

(in terror)

Don't play something I like -- play something he likes!!

HIRAM

I'll try him on Stephen Foster.

Hiram puts the comb to his lips and roughing out a version of "Jeannie with the Light Brown Hair."

MED. SHOT-GROUP

The Headmaster, Ernie and Ada are grouped close together and staring at the cobra as Hiram plays.

CLOSE SHOT-BASKET

The cobra is swaying back and forth.

CLOSE SHOT-HIRAM

His head is also swaying as he plays.

MED. SHOT-COMPARTMENT

Hiram slowly approaches the basket as he plays. The cobra is now slowly lowering itself back into the basket. Hiram comes to the end of the tune and he quickly flips the lid of the basket down on the snake. With his other hand, he carefully returns the comb to his pocket.

FULL SHOT-COMPARTMENT

The others relax somewhat.

ADA

You did it!

HIRAM

(thoughtfully)

I'd like to try him on "Camptown Races."

HEADMASTER

No!!!!!

HIRAM

Some other time, then. Now if you don't mind leaving...

HEADMASTER

(sharply)

Ernie.

Ernie steps over in front of the door with his knife ready. Hiram counters by picking up the basket. Ernie backs off quickly.

ERNIE

Keep that thing in there!

Hiram walks to the door carrying the basket. He pauses at the door.

HIRAM

I have a slight confession to make. The music was merely a theatrical touch. Most authorities agree it's the rhythmic swaying of the head which immobilizes the snake.

CLOSE SHOT-HIRAM

He sways his head slightly from side to side.

MED. SHOT-GROUP

They sway in reaction to Hiram.

FULL SHOT-COMPARTMENT

HIRAM

(continuing)

I have no recourse but to take this up with the authorities.

The group stares at him as Hiram goes out the door.

MED. SHOT-CORRIDOR

Carrying the basket, Hiram works his way along the corridor CAMERA MOVING with him.

FULL SHOT-DINING CAR

Joel Smith is finishing his dinner as Hiram comes into the picture. Joel looks up and stares.

> HIRAM
> (not pausing)

Hi, Joel.

He goes on by as Joel swivels around and stares after him.

MED. SHOT-CORRIDOR

Hiram stops at the door of the Bobby's compartment and knocks.

MED. SHOT-BOBBY'S COMPARTMENT

The Bobby is relaxed with his shoes off and peeling an apple with his pocketknife. He looks up as Hiram knocks.

> BOBBY

Shove off!

Hiram opens the door and comes in.

> HIRAM

Guess what's in the basket?

> BOBBY

The cobra.

> HIRAM

How did you know?

BOBBY

How did I know? How did I know Bob's your uncle?

Hiram is a little hurt.

HIRAM

I think you doubt my veracity.

BOBBY

(wearily)

All right, open it up and let me have a look at your prize.

HIRAM

He's also trying to steal the Shahbandar diamond. That's the diamond that the cobra here is guarding. Kala Nag, that's his name. The cobra that is.

BOBBY

What's your name?

HIRAM

Holliday. Hiram Holliday.

BOBBY

Well, Mr. Holliday let's go.

HIRAM

Of course.

The Bobby pulls his shoes on and he follows Hiram out the compartment.

FULL SHOT-DINING CAR

Joel Smith is sipping his coffee as Hiram comes by, still carrying the basket and followed by the Bobby.

HIRAM

Hello, Joel.

Joel does another take.

MED. SHOT-CORRIDOR

Hiram leads the way down the corridor with the Bobby behind him. CAMERA MOVES with them. At the door of Hiram's compartment, the Bobby stops him.

BOBBY

Far enough, Mr. Holliday.

HIRAM

But the Headmaster's compartment is down here.

He gestures.

BOBBY

Never mind the Headmaster. In you go.

He propels Hiram into his compartment.

MED. SHOT-COMPARTMENT

Hiram enters, trips over something on the floor and almost loses the basket, retrieving it at the last moment.

BOBBY

You want to be more careful the way you handle cobras.

HIRAM

But the Headmaster...

BOBBY

I've been very patient with you, Mr. Holliday. But my capacity's been reached and over reached. At the next stop you, your snake, your dead 'Indoo' and your diamond are all going to get off. Enjoy real English hospitality until all these here apparitions crawl back in the woodwork!

HIRAM

But...

BOBBY

Next stop and don't stick your head out of this door between now and then!

He goes out, closing the door vigorously. Trying to reassure himself of the reality of the situation, Hiram takes a small peek inside the basket then slams the lid down again hastily. He sits down on the basket to think, then looks up as he hears someone at the door.

CLOSE SHOT-AT DOOR

Ada slips in quickly then pauses at the door as she looks back down the corridor and to make sure she has not been seen.

MED. SHOT-COMPARTMENT

HIRAM

Come in, I hope you'll pardon me for not rising.

The girl comes to him quickly.

                              ADA

Hiram Holliday, you must help me!

She takes hold of his lapels and pulls him up close to her. He manages to put a prudent foot on the top of the basket.

                            HIRAM

Now, what can I do for you?

                              ADA

I have the Shahbandar! The Headmaster suspects that I have crossed him. I need someone on my side, someone brave and powerful.

                            HIRAM

                          (politely)

Do you have anyone in mind?

                              ADA

You, Hiram.

Hiram sits down on the basket again and suddenly Ada kneels beside him.

                              ADA

Half of the Shahbandar...

                    (hands him the gem)

...all of me.

CLOSE SHOT-AT DOOR

The Headmaster stands at the door with a gun in his hand.

HEADMASTER

I should not advise you to accept, Mr. Holliday.

FULL SHOT-COMPARTMENT

Ada stands up.

ADA

You.

HEADMASTER

In the long run, Ada is much more deadly than Kala Nag. The Shahbandar, please.

He advances holding out his hand.

HIRAM

I'm afraid you will only have custody until the next station.

HEADMASTER

You underestimate us. The train will not reach the next station. Ernest has gone forward to take over from the engineer. The Shahbandar.

The Headmaster comes forward and Hiram suddenly grabs his umbrella, thrusting the tip into the Headmaster's gun barrel.

CLOSE SHOT-GUN

The gun barrel explodes as the Headmaster pulls the trigger.

FULL SHOT-COMPARTMENT

The Headmaster cries out in pain, shaking his hand as Hiram dashes past him out the door.

MED. SHOT-CORRIDOR

Hiram dashes a few steps down the corridor past the Headmaster's compartment and then stops short.

CORRIDOR -- HIRAM'S POV

The Bobby is standing in the corridor cleaning his nails with his pocket knife.

MED. SHOT-HIRAM'S COMPARTMENT

The Headmaster now has his cane which he quickly reveals as a sword cane. He dashes to the door as the girl cowers in the corner and heads in the direction opposite the one taken by Hiram.

MED. SHOT-CORRIDOR

The Headmaster hurries along the corridor, CAMERA MOVING with him, Hiram comes up behind him, reverses his umbrella, and hooks the Headmaster's foot. The Headmaster goes down heavily and Hiram goes over him and stepping on his back in the narrow corridor.

CLOSE SHOT -- ON FLOOR

The Headmaster gets Hiram's foot in the back and his face hits the floor.

FULL SHOT -- DINING CAR

Joel looks up as Hiram speeds past him. Joel is half getting up when he is knocked back by the Headmaster, who is pursuing Hiram. He then gets up and is moving out into the aisle when he becomes involved in a violent collision with the Bobby who is hurrying after Hiram and the Headmaster. Joel and the Bobby go down in a tangle.

CLOSE SHOT -- ERNIE

Suddenly the crook of Hiram's umbrella comes into the picture and hooks around his neck and jerking him backward violently.

WIDER ANGLE

Hiram tries to get past the fallen Ernie. Ernie rises and advances on Hiram. Just as he is taking a wicked swing at Hiram, the train lurches and Ernie misses. Hiram sees the danger and whirls around. By this time the Headmaster enters the baggage car, both he and Ernie close in on Hiram. The two advance on Hiram, aiming blows at him which he parries as best as he can with his umbrella, but is forced back quickly toward the door. When it looks like his doom is certain he quickly steps through the door to the outside of the train.

FULL SHOT-TOP OF TRAIN

Hiram climbs up on top of the engine and retreats to the rear over the top of a car. He is followed closely by first Ernie with his axe and then the Headmaster.

MED. SHOT -- TOP OF CAR

Ernie advances on Hiram, aiming murderous blows with his axe. Hiram parries but each blow causes his umbrella to lose some of its length. (INTER CUT CLOSE SHOTS.) Hiram is finally left with little more than a handle, and Ernie and the Headmaster are pressing him closely. Ernie aims what should be the final swing. Hiram suddenly reaches up and hooks an overhead wire, flying up in the air and away from the two.

FULL SHOT – HIRAM -- OTHERS' POV

He is hanging onto a "telltale" wire with his umbrella handle.

FULL SHOT-TRAIN-GROUND POV

The train is entering a tunnel as the two on top of the train still stare after Hiram, hanging between two uprights along the track. The tunnel catches the two completely unaware.

CLOSE SHOT -- HIRAM

He looks after the train, then looks down and up again quickly.

INT. CAB -- FULL SHOT

The engineer has regained his feet and heads for the controls.

DISSOLVE:

INT. HIRAM'S COMPARTMENT – NIGHT -- FULL SHOT

Hiram and Joel are sitting in their compartment, which is now back in order. The Bobby is at the door ready to go.

> BOBBY

All secure now, Mr. Holliday. The locals will take off the girl and what's left of those two chaps at the next station.

> HIRAM

Thank you.

> BOBBY

And, Mr. Holliday...

> HIRAM

Yes?

> BOBBY

I knew all along you were a bit of all right. Goodnight, sir.

With a salute to Hiram, he leaves.

> SMITH

Hiram...why on earth didn't you let me know all this was happening?

HIRAM

I didn't want to disturb you while you were eating.

SMITH

Oh...Hiram, you've simply got to stop taking all these chances. Do you know what it could have cost you?

HIRAM

Indeed I do.

(displays tattered remains of his umbrella)

Look what happened to my umbrella!

He tries to open it. Joel stares at him for a moment, then rises, and starts out.

INT. CORRIDOR-CLOSE SHOT-SMITH

He enters and leans against the wall.

SMITH

(into CAMERA)

I'm worried about his life. He's worried about his umbrella! Well, that's Hiram Holliday. Let's see how Bonnie Scotland will like him.

FADE OUT

THE END

The Adventure of the False Monarch

This was the third script to be commissioned and, indeed, the third episode to air, with NBC showing it on 17 October 1956. It first ran on the BBC on 4 August 1960 and was repeated on 5 February the following year. It was written, produced and directed by the show's creator, Phil Rapp. The cast in this episode included Richard Aherne as the Earl, Angela Greene as the Queen of Rovakia and Thurston Hall as Harrison Prentice.

FADE IN:

EXT. SCOTTISH VILLAGE-DAY - (STOCK) - ESTABLISHING SHOT

CAMERA ZOOMS IN on the hanging sign of the village hotel. It reads: "Loch Dunoon Inn."

DISSOLVE THRU:

INT. INN-DAY-FULL SHOT

This is the common room of the inn, with a few diners seated at tables to one side. One of the diners enjoying his food is JOEL SMITH. A porter comes by Joel's table carrying some bags, followed by HARRISON PRENTICE, who sees Joel and stops.

PRENTICE

Smith! I've been chasing you all over Scotland! How do you expect me to publish the Sentinel and play bloodhound at the same time!

JOEL

(starting)

I thought you were in New York.

PRENTICE

Oh, you did.

He sits down at the table, seething.

TWO SHOT-JOEL AND PRENTICE

PRENTICE

(continuing)

Where is he? Have you lost him again?

JOEL

Lost who, Mr. Prentice?

Prentice gives him a withering look.

PRENTICE

Only the man I sent you abroad with, Smith. Only the man whose story I assigned you to get. Only the most sensational news source of our time, that's all. Where is Hiram Holliday???

JOEL

I think he's out gathering lichens.

PRENTICE

Lichens?? You mean fungus?

JOEL

He says Scotland has some dandy specimens.

PRENTICE

Smith, you're not only a miserable reporter–you're a gullible fool! Hiram Holliday is not out looking for lichens!

JOEL
(trying to calm him)

How about some food, Mr. Prentice?

He starts to eat again.

PRENTICE

I haven't been able to eat since I left New York! Wondering what Holliday is up to, and what new way you'll find to miss the entire story!

JOEL

But he said he was just...

PRENTICE

That's what he tells you. In Paris, he fought a duel on a high wire against an assassin armed with two rapiers. What did he tell you? He was hunting truffles!

JOEL

But...

PRENTICE

In London, he recovered the world's most valuable diamond by charming a cobra with a comb and tissue paper, and where did you think he was? Out looking for igneous rocks!

JOEL
(mouth full)

No, I....

PRENTICE

This man is not a fungus hunter, Smith! While you sit here, stuffing your face, a Knight of the Round Table is out questing adventure!

JOEL

Hiram Holliday?

PRENTICE

Hiram Holliday!

INT. HALLWAY OF INN-FULL SHOT

This is the upstairs hallway of the inn. Walking TOWARD CAMERA is HIRAM, who has just come in from the outside. He has a knapsack over his shoulder and as he walks, he is looking through a magnifying glass at a lichen he holds in his other hand. In front of him, a man emerges from a door, closes the door, turns and bumps into Hiram, neither one seeing the other in time to avoid a minor collision.

HIRAM

Say! That was clumsy of me.

ULRICH

It was my fault, your maj...

He breaks off and stares.

TWO SHOT -- ULRICH AND HIRAM

ULRICH, who is a minister from a small Middle-European country and carries a slight accent of an indeterminate kind, is looking at Hiram in complete confusion, as Hiram smiles back politely.

ULRICH

Did not I just leave you in that room?

HIRAM

I don't believe so. I just came up the back stairway. I was out gathering lichens.

Ulrich continues to stare.

ULRICH

You are not...? You must be. But you are not.

HIRAM

The name is Hiram Holliday.

(displaying plant)

This is the lichen.

ULRICH
(shaking his head)

Amazing. Amazing.

HIRAM

Yes, isn't it? A prime specimen of Cladonia rangiferina, highly esteemed by caribou.

He holds up the lichen to which Ulrich pays no attention.

ULRICH

Enough like him to be a twin.

HIRAM

The resemblance to Parmelia is quite strong. The caribou, however, is seldom deceived.

Ulrich comes to a quick decision.

ULRICH

You will do me the favor, sir, of remaining here for one moment? I assure you, it is of the utmost, of the gravest importance.

                         HIRAM

Here?

                         ULRICH

Here.

He turns back to the door through which he has just come, then turns back for another look at Hiram.

                         ULRICH

    Amazing

He goes through the door, closing it behind him.

CLOSE SHOT - HIRAM

He looks after Ulrich, then does a slightly puzzled shrug.

INT. KING'S ROOM - FULL SHOT

CAMERA IS SHOOTING TOWARD the door, over the shoulder of a man seated in a chair. Ulrich stands at the door.

                         ULRICH

    Your majesty.

The man in the chair speaks with a clipped British accent. This is KING SIEGFRIED THE FIRST, Oxford-educated King of Rovakia.

                         SIEGFRIED

You enter without knocking?

                         ULRICH

Pardon, sire. But there stands without the sudden, heaven-sent answer to our problem.

SIEGFRIED

You are dramatic, Ulrich.

ULRICH

But not without reason.

He advances into the room and assumes a more confidential tone.

ULRICH

We suspect, sire, an attempt will be made on your life should you spend the weekend at Castle McConkie. But how to make the enemy show his hand without danger to the royal personage?

SIEGFRIED
(ironically)

How, indeed.

ULRICH

But if a double were to go in your stead?

ULRICH
(gesturing)

Outside. An American. Hiram Holliday.

SIEGFRIED

He would chance it? To take my place?

ULRICH

If your majesty would permit me to handle that aspect...

SIEGFRIED

And the Queen? She arrives at the castle tonight...would she be told?

ULRICH

I think it more prudent not.

(as Siegfried reacts; anticipating
Siegfried's reaction, quickly continues)

We must assume him to be a man of honor. And for your country...

SIEGFRIED
(rising)

For Rovakia, no sacrifice is too great. Bring in your Mr. Holliday, Ulrich. I will wait in the other room and observe.

The king goes toward the door leading to a connecting room. At the door, he turns and we see his face for the first time. Although he wears a monocle and has a royal crest on his robe, the resemblance to Hiram is physically complete.

SIEGFRIED

(shaking his head)

A double for me? Fantastic!

He goes into the other room, leaving the door slightly ajar. Ulrich goes to the door leading to the hall, opening it.

INT. HALLWAY-MED. SHOT

Hiram is studying his lichen as the door opens.

ULRICH

Would you come in, Mr. Holliday?

HIRAM

Thank you.

(showing plant)

You were right. This is Parmelia. Having no caribou blood I was deceived.

He gives a breathy little laugh and goes through the door.

INT. ROOM-FULL SHOT

Ulrich closes the door behind Hiram, then motions him toward the chair recently vacated by Siegfried.

ULRICH

Would you please sit down...there?

Hiram goes to the chair and sits. He is facing the door which connects with the other room and which is still slightly ajar.

ULRICH
(continuing)

Comfortable?

CLOSE SHOT - HIRAM

As he settles in the chair.

HIRAM

Quite. It seems to have been kept warm.

CLOSE SHOT - HIRAM

His face just partially revealed through crack in door. He appears stunned, his monocle drops from his eye.

FULL SHOT - ROOM

Ulrich comes closer but is careful not to get in the line of vision of the king.

TWO SHOT - ULRICH AND HIRAM

ULRICH

I come quickly to the point, as you say in America. You are familiar with Siegfried the First, of Rovakia?

HIRAM

Not exactly, no.

ULRICH

The king is ill, Mr. Holliday. Back home, his enemies would use this to usurp the throne.

HIRAM

I'm terribly sorry.

ULRICH

To thwart their evil schemes, it is most important that the king appear this weekend at nearby McConkie Castle, vigorous and glowing with health.

HIRAM

(starting to rise)

I have some vitamin pills in my room...

ULRICH

No. He can appear, Mr. Holliday...he must. The decision is yours.

HIRAM
(sits again)

Mine?

ULRICH

You, Hiram Holliday, are enough like Siegfried the First to be his twin.

CLOSE SHOT - SIEGFRIED

He sniffs deprecatingly.

HIRAM'S VOICE

Say, isn't that a coincidence.

ULRICH

On behalf of the Rovakian people I ask you to spend this weekend as Siegfried the First. Our country, though poor, will meet any price you name.

HIRAM

I couldn't think of doing it for money.

ULRICH

What then?

HIRAM

(ponders for a few seconds)

Well, there are some rare lichens inside the north wall of the castle–and I've been unable to get past the guards.

ULRICH

Then we kill two birds with one stone! And you will say no word to anyone of this. Anyone.

HIRAM

Naturally.

ULRICH

Hiram Holliday...you sat as a commoner, you arise a king.

He takes Hiram's hand, assisting him in rising. He then bows over the hand.

HIRAM

You know, I find this most peculiar.

ULRICH

Yes, majesty?

HIRAM

I am not intellectually impressed by the system of monarchial government, yet when I receive this regal attention, I notice in myself a rapid acceleration of the heartbeat.

ULRICH

That, sir, is a condition which will pass...quite suddenly.

WIPE TO:

INT. INN-DAY-MED. SHOT-JOEL AND PRENTICE

Prentice is looking impatiently at his watch; Joel is still stowing away the food.

PRENTICE

(irritated)

Well, where is he, Smith? How can you keep on shovelling in that food when you don't know what's happened to Hiram!

JOEL

Mr. Prentice...what can happen to Hiram gathering lichens?

PRENTICE
(snorts)

Lichens! Why do you fall for...?

JOEL
(hastily)

I think you ought to eat, Mr. Prentice. The food's very good here.

PRENTICE

What's that you're eating?

JOEL

Haggis. I have it every morning. It's delicious.

PRENTICE

Haggis?

JOEL

Made from the liver and lungs of a sheep, minced with oatmeal, onions and suet and boiled in the sheep's own stomach. Would you like to try some?

PRENTICE
(weakly)

You're insane. Now I know why Holliday–

He breaks off, staring off scene.

JOEL

What's the matter?

He swivels around to see.

FULL SHOT-INN

Hiram, dressed in a cutaway and with a row of ribbons decorating it but still carrying his umbrella on one arm, is at the head of a small procession consisting of Ulrich and two burly footmen. CAMERA TRUCKS with him as he walks. He passes the table of Joel and Prentice without stopping but nods pleasantly.

HIRAM

Hello, Joel. Mr. Prentice! Welcome to Scotland. Good day.

The procession passes on, CAMERA STAYING with Joel and Prentice who are staring after Hiram.

PRENTICE

Who...who are those people? Why is he dressed like that?

Joel gives a helpless shrug.

PRENTICE

(continuing)

Come on!

He gets up suddenly, Joel following, and starts after Hiram.

PRENTICE

(continuing)

Holliday! Hiram! Wait!

The two footmen turn back to meet them, firmly taking Prentice and Joel by the backs of their collars and pants and forcibly escorting them back to their chairs and seating them. The footmen then march off decorously.

MED. SHOT-AT TABLE

A WAITER moves to the table as Joel and Prentice are sitting, stunned.

PRENTICE

(to waiter)

Why did they do that?

WAITER

(Scottish)

They don't like anyone getting too close to his majesty.

PRENTICE

His majesty?

WAITER

The King of Rovakia...Siegfried the First.

JOEL

Siegfried the First??

WAITER

On his way to McConkie Castle.

(lowers voice)

They say he's meeting the beautiful queen there tonight.

The waiter moves off as Prentice looks at Joel.

PRENTICE

(burning)

Out gathering lichens...! Smith, you're fired!

DISSOLVE:

EXT. SCOTTISH CASTLE-DAY - (STOCK) - ESTABLISHING SHOT

This should, if possible, give also some picture of the Scottish landscape as well as the castle.

INT. CASTLE ENTRANCE HALL-FULL VIEW

CAMERA PANS the large entrance hall, STOPPING ON a welcoming party consisting of the EARL OF McCONKIE, his castle staff, and two kilted pipers who are BLOWING A WELCOME to the visiting monarch. Hiram and his retinue enter the scene and the pipers wind up with a final skirl. The Earl advances to meet Hiram. He has no trace of a Scottish accent and is dressed impeccable in tails.

MED. SHOT-GROUP

EARL

Your majesty, the Castle McConkie and all within its walls belong to you.

HIRAM

That's certainly most generous.

Ulrich steps forward to make the introduction.

ULRICH

Your imperial majesty, the 26th Earl of McConkie.

Hiram puts out his hand, which the Earl takes with both of his and bows over.

EARL

A great day for the Clan McConkie.

HIRAM

Very nice place you have here.

EARL

Since 1071 the guardian to Ballachulish and the Firth of Lorn.

HIRAM

(rapping a wall with his umbrella)

They certainly built them right in those days.

EARL

If you will step this way, your majesty...

He leads Hiram down the hall with a retinue following. CAMERA PANS with them. They halt before a large portrait on the wall.

EARL

(continuing)

Here, the 25th Earl of McConkie.

MED. SHOT - PAINTING

It depicts a seated nobleman in tartan, etc.

TWO SHOT - HIRAM AND EARL

EARL

(continuing)

I think the light is better from here, highness.

He carefully moves Hiram a few inches to one side.

EARL

(continuing)

Perfect.

He moves slightly away from Hiram, glances off, gives an almost imperceptible signal with his eyes.

CLOSE SHOT - ARROW SLIT

Set in wall of castle. The barb of an arrow can be seen in the aperture.

MED. SHOT - AT PAINTING

CAMERA IS SHOOTING over Hiram's shoulder at picture. An enormous arrow suddenly whizzes past Hiram's ear and buries itself in the chest of the 25th Earl. Hiram walks to the picture, removes the arrow, and then turns.

HIRAM

I believe the castle is besieged.

CLOSE SHOT - EARL

He looks off, a brief flicker of annoyance at the miss.

CLOSE SHOT - ULRICH

Astounded at Hiram's coolness.

GROUP SHOT

The Earl moves to Hiram.

EARL

It came through the arrow slit...a careless rabbit hunter! Are you all right, majesty?

HIRAM

Oh, I'm just fine.

He looks at the arrow, taking in its size.

HIRAM

(continuing)

But I should hate to meet one of your rabbits.

EARL

That the McConkie tartan might have been stained with the royal blood...this could never be erased.

ULRICH

(coldly)

May I suggest we move on?

He casts an apprehensive eye in the direction of the arrow slit.

EARL

Of course.

They move down the hall, CAMERA TRUCKING with them. They halt before a mounted suit of armor, standing on a platform against the wall. A murderous battle axe is raised over the head and held with both hands.

EARL

(continuing)

The first McConkie. As he was in 1072, when alone he held this very hall against a savage horde from the Lowlands.

HIRAM

Oh yes–I've read about him. Wee Jock McConkie. It's said he cut off the sporrans of eight members of the McFarkle clan with a single blow of his claymore!

EARL

Right in the spot where you stand, your majesty.

(judiciously)

Or perhaps a pace to the right.

Hiram takes a step over, placing himself directly in the line of the axe, should it fall.

HIRAM

Here?

EARL

There.

The axe appears to sway a trifle and Ulrich leaps forward, clutching at Hiram.

ULRICH

(pulling him to one side)

May I counsel that his highness be shown to his chambers, before another...ah...accident?

HIRAM

Chambers? Would it be convenient if they faced the North Wall?

EARL

As you wish. Perhaps a rest before the banquet tonight.

ULRICH

An excellent suggestion. You may lead the way, sir.

The Earl shoots him a searching glance then starts ahead. As the procession follows, the skirling of the bagpipes is HEARD.

DISSOLVE:

INT. BANQUET HALL-NIGHT - FULL SHOT

A banquet is in progress, with Hiram in the place of honor at the head of the table, flanked by the Earl and Ulrich. The two pipers, kilted in the McConkie Tartan, are playing their bagpipes, as an attractive Scottish girl, also in kilts, dances the traditional sword dance.

MED. SHOT-HEAD OF TABLE

The Earl turns to Hiram, who keeps looking up nervously.

EARL

Enjoying yourself, majesty?

HIRAM

Oh, immensely!

Hiram looks up again. CAMERA FOLLOWS his gaze, revealing a huge sword suspended just above Hiram's head, and hanging by a very thin cord. CAMERA PANS DOWN again. Hiram looks to the Earl, who has apparently not noticed his upward glance.

MED. SHOT-DANCER

She is performing the intricate steps over the crossed swords.

MED. SHOT - AT TABLE

As Ulrich and the Earl watch the dance, Hiram sneaks another peek above.

CLOSE SHOT - STRING

The string suspending it is starting to unravel.

AT TABLE

Hiram, more apprehensive now, wishes that the Earl would notice and explain the sword above his head, but the Earl is intent on the dance. Hiram shrugs, then watches the dance.

FULL SHOT - HALL

The girl finishes the dance, takes her bow and goes off, as two kilted jugglers carrying knives follow her on. Hiram applauds politely, at the same time sneaking a few glances above. The jugglers start to throw the knives back and forth to one another, in quickening tempo.

AT TABLE

Hiram takes another look up.

CLOSE SHOT - SWORD

The string is unraveled down to a thread.

TWO SHOT - HIRAM AND EARL

Hiram looks down from the sword, then taps the Earl lightly on the shoulder. The Earl turns to him.

HIRAM

While I don't wish to appear impolite, there is something I am a little curious about.

EARL

(discreetly)

The girl, your highness?

HIRAM

No - that!

He points up. The Earl follows his gaze.

CLOSE SHOT - SWORD

It seems about to fall.

TWO SHOT - HIRAM AND EARL

EARL

The Sword of McConkie. But your highness may rest easy.

HIRAM

Oh?

EARL

Tradition says the sword shall only fall if the chair below is taken by a false monarch.

He smiles at Hiram. Hiram digests this information for a brief moment, then starts up violently.

CLOSE SHOT - SEAT

The sword falls, going right through the seat of the chair and burying its point in the floor beneath.

FULL SHOT - HALL

Hiram has propelled himself forward into the line of fire of the two knife-throwers. Knives are whizzing all around him.

CLOSE SHOT - HIRAM

In self-defense, he catches one knife, then another. Like a shortstop flagging down a multitude of batted balls, Hiram catches the knives at all angles, until he has them all.

FULL SHOT - HALL

All are staring at Hiram, who is standing holding the knives.

EARL

Magnificent! A magnificent performance!

CLOSE SHOT - HIRAM

HIRAM

Thank you. Sometime I'd like to try it with real knives.

He drops the knives, which all stick quivering in the floor.

HIRAM

(continuing; looks down, shakes his head)

I may have to give up collecting lichens.

FADE OUT

END OF ACT ONE

ACT TWO

FADE IN:

INT. ROYAL CHAMBERS-NIGHT - FULL SHOT

Hiram, in pyjamas and robe, is testing a canopied bed with his hand as Ulrich stands by the door, ready to be dismissed for the night.

ULRICH

Will there be anything else tonight, your majesty?

HIRAM

I don't believe so. But, Ulrich...

ULRICH

Sire?

Hiram comes over to him.

HIRAM

It's not that I have anything against Siegfried the First, but when we're alone I'd appreciate being referred to as Hiram Holliday. It seems to fit me better.

ULRICH

Certainly. No one here suspects your true identity.

HIRAM

It may be just a silly idea, but do you think the Earl of McConkie has sort of a grudge against Siegfried?

ULRICH

Remember only that you are performing a service for which Rovakia will be in your debt forever. Sleep well, Hiram Holliday.

He goes out, closing the door.

CLOSE SHOT - HIRAM

He sits down on the bed and starts taking off his slippers. There is a CREAKING NOISE off. Hiram listens, then turns around.

CLOSE SHOT-DOOR

This is a door leading to another chamber. The latch is slowly turning, making the CREAKING SOUND.

FULL SHOT - ROOM

Hiram rises silently from the bed, picking up his umbrella. He tiptoes over to the door, which is now slowly opening.

MED. SHOT - AT DOOR

Hiram stands by with his umbrella at the ready. Through the door comes a beautiful and regal WOMAN, with a robe over her nightgown.

> QUEEN

Good evening, Siegfried.

> HIRAM

Oh...how do you do? I...wasn't expecting company.

She looks at the umbrella.

> QUEEN

You were expecting rain?

> HIRAM

Just in case I walk in my sleep.

Embarrassed, he attempts to carry it off by twirling the umbrella, but drops it and has to pick it up again. The Queen looks at him closely.

> QUEEN

Do you feel all right, darling?

The "darling" startles him again.

HIRAM

Are you sure you ought to be here?

LARGER ANGLE - ROOM

Hiram is retreating slightly.

QUEEN

Of course. You instructed me to join you here tonight. I just arrived.

HIRAM

Oh. Well, I guess that clears up everything, except for one small point.

QUEEN

And that is?

HIRAM

Who are you?

QUEEN

You jest, Siegfried. Not even you can be so cruel. You deny your queen?

HIRAM

Queen?

QUEEN

Yours to command.

She bows her head. Hiram, who has by this time retreated to the bed, sits down to think it over.

CLOSE SHOT - HIRAM

> HIRAM

Well now.

EXT. WALL OF CASTLE - NIGHT-FULL SHOT

Two figures are walking furtively along the darkened wall. There is a muttered exclamation as one of them stubs his toe on a large rock. The other lights a cigarette lighter and we can see it is Joel. Prentice is holding his foot.

> JOEL

Shh!

TWO SHOT - JOEL AND PRENTICE

> PRENTICE

> (testily)

Just mind your own business, Smith.

> JOEL

I still don't think we should be prowling around here, Mr Prentice.

> PRENTICE

Oh, you don't. Isn't this where Hiram Holliday went? Then this is where the story is and this is one time I'm going to see that we get it!

> JOEL

Yes, sir.

PRENTICE

Now, let's go.

WIDER ANGLE

As Prentice and Joel proceed down along the wall, two guards sneak up from behind and jump them, bearing them down to the ground.

INT. ROYAL CHAMBERS - MED. SHOT

Hiram is still seated on the royal bed, with the queen now seated beside him, looking deep into his eyes.

QUEEN

Siegfried. Somehow you seem so strange...so changed. You're not the same man I married.

HIRAM

Madam, you have scored a bulls-eye.

He endeavours to move away, but she has his hands and holds him tight.

QUEEN

The face is the same but the eyes...the eyes are kinder.

HIRAM

I believe you had best return to your own chambers.

QUEEN

Do not send me away, Siegfried! Not again! No!

There is the SOUND of a scuffle in the hall outside.

HIRAM

Excuse me.

He goes to the door leading to the hall, opens it and looks out.

INT. HALL-FULL SHOT

Joel and Prentice are being dragged along by two burly guards. They see Hiram.

PRENTICE

Holliday! Do something! They're throwing us in the dungeon!

JOEL

They're going to lock us up!

They are dragged past as Hiram looks after them. He closes the door.

INT. ROYAL CHAMBERS - FULL SHOT

QUEEN

What was that?

HIRAM

A slight emergency of state has arisen. It will require my attention for a few minutes.

QUEEN

Let me go with you, Siegfried! Let me share your life! Let me help you!

HIRAM

I believe you can. Do you happen to have a Bobby-pin?

QUICK DISSOLVE:

INT. DUNGEON-FULL SHOT

Prentice and Joel are seated disconsolately on the floor, leaning back against the wall.

PRENTICE

What do you suppose they're going to do with us, Smith?

JOEL

I don't know. I don't know what Hiram is doing here and I don't know what I'm doing here.

PRENTICE

I'll notify the American consulate!

JOEL

With what? Smoke signals?

Prentice hears something.

PRENTICE

What was that?

JOEL

Sounded like someone at the door.

PRENTICE

Sell your life dearly, Smith!

Joel looks at him.

JOEL

What about you?

PRENTICE

I shall wrap myself in the American flag.

The door CREAKS open and Hiram steps in, smiling. He carries his umbrella but is still in his robe.

HIRAM

How do you do, gentlemen?

JOEL

Hiram!

PRENTICE

How did you open the door?

HIRAM

I have made a study, although not for commercial purposes, of the fine art of lock-picking.

(holds up Bobby pin)

As a matter of fact, the treasures of antiquity would be helpless before a man equipped with a Bobby pin, and...

PRENTICE

Yes. But can you get us out of here?

HIRAM

Just follow me.

He turns and goes out the door with the other two following.

INT. HALLWAY-FULL SHOT

The three tiptoe down the hallway with Hiram in the lead and Joel bringing up the rear. All are looking around warily. Seemingly hearing a noise, all flatten against the wall. The part of the wall against which Joel is leaning revolves suddenly and he disappears on the other side as Prentice reaches back for him.

PRENTICE

Keep close, Smith. Don't dawdle.

He waves his hands in the air, feeling nothing. Hiram and Prentice turn around to find themselves alone.

PRENTICE

(continuing)

Smith? Smith?

HIRAM

Where did he go?

PRENTICE

I never saw such a man for wandering off somewhere! Come on, Holliday!

Hiram peers around for Joel but not finding him, starts off again. CAMERA TRUCKS with them. They pass the door to the royal chambers. Prentice points to it.

PRENTICE

(continuing)

What's in there?

> HIRAM

The royal chambers.

> PRENTICE

Would it be safe?

> HIRAM

> (considering)

I do not believe so.

He stops Prentice suddenly, looking ahead.

LONG VIEW - CORRIDOR

Two guards are searching the corridor.

MED. SHOT - HALL

> HIRAM

> (continuing)

In here.

He quickly leads Prentice through a door opposite the royal chambers.

INT. TORTURE CHAMBER - REVERSE SHOT - DOOR

Hiram and Prentice enter, close the door and listen intently, then relax.

> PRENTICE

Safe.

His eyes roam around the room and he starts.

FULL SHOT-ROOM - PRENTICE'S POV

They are in what is the torture chamber of the castle, with various medieval instruments of torture arrayed about the room.

MED. SHOT - AT DOOR

PRENTICE

(continuing)

It's the torture chamber! Let's get out of here!

He turns and tries the door but it is bolted from the other side.

PRENTICE

(continuing)

It's locked! From the outside!

HIRAM

This could be serious...I've mislaid my Bobby pin.

PRENTICE

Holliday, what's this all about? First you're out hunting lichens, then you're masquerading as a king, and now we end up in a torture chamber! What's going on??

HIRAM

I regret to say, Mr. Prentice, that I cannot give out the information.

PRENTICE

Holliday!

FULL SHOT - ROOM

Hiram walks around, looking at the various equipment.

> PRENTICE
>
> (continuing)

What's that?

Hiram is looking at a large wooden frame.

> HIRAM

A rack. Also known as the Duke of Exeter's daughter, because of its introduction in England by that gentleman. It stretches the human body to quite disproportionate lengths.

> PRENTICE

We've got to get out of here!

> HIRAM

Say, did you ever see such a handsome thumb-screw?

> PRENTICE

Stop talking that way!

Hiram has now halted before a guillotine.

> HIRAM

Here's another interesting specimen.

> PRENTICE

I'd stay away from that, Holliday.

> HIRAM

Most likely hasn't been used in several hundred years.

He gets down on his knees to examine the mechanism.

CLOSER ANGLE - GUILLOTINE

As Hiram has his neck forward, looking over the block, the knife falls suddenly. At that instant, Hiram puts up the umbrella and stops the knife just above his neck, in the manner of propping up a window.

PRENTICE'S VOICE (o.s.)

Holliday!

FULL SHOT - ROOM

Hiram reaches up and feels the blade with his finger.

HIRAM

Oooh. Sharp.

He rises, leaving his umbrella holding up the blade.

PRENTICE

Holliday, someone is out to kill us!

HIRAM

Mr. Prentice, the series of events forces me to agree that you may be right.

PRENTICE

But why? Why?

HIRAM

The King of Rovakia seems to have aroused ill-feelings in certain quarters.

PRENTICE

But what has that got to do with us??

HIRAM

(looking off)

I believe we are having a manifestation.

Prentice follows his gaze.

CLOSER SHOT - BOOK AND CANDLE

An opened book with a lighted candle beside it are floating through the air toward Hiram and Prentice.

FULL SHOT - ROOM

PRENTICE

It's floating through the air!

HIRAM

Don't be alarmed, Mr. Prentice. A rather crude attempt at intimidation. The book and candle are merely suspended on wires. Watch.

He steps forward and waves his arms above the candle and book, but finds no wires.

PRENTICE

(in horror)

Holliday!

HIRAM

(thoughtfully)

I wonder how they do that?

He takes hold of the book and looks at it, also holding the candle for light.

PRENTICE

Wh-what does it say?

HIRAM

An account of the 13th McConkie, beheaded in 1402.

PRENTICE

Beheaded?

HIRAM

In the torture chamber of the castle.

PRENTICE

That's this room!

HIRAM

Yes.

(reads on)

It seems that from that time hence the gentleman has been known as the McConkie ghost, wandering about head in hand, so to speak.

PRENTICE

Is he a...friendly ghost?

HIRAM

Excuse me.

He hands Prentice the candle while he turns the page. He reads a few words, then turns to Prentice.

HIRAM

(continuing)

It would seem not.

As Prentice stares at Hiram, a CREAKING SOUND is heard. Both turn to the wall where a panel is slowly yawning open.

MED. CLOSE SHOT - AT WALL

Through the opening in the wall slowly walks a figure in chain mail and breastplate, carrying a large and evil-looking mace. The figure is carrying in the other hand a helmet, being apparently headless.

FULL SHOT - ROOM

Prentice, with a gentle moan, sinks to the floor, dropping the candle, and lies in a dead faint. Hiram looks at him, then looks at the figure in armour.

HIRAM

Won't you come in?

The figure stalks slowly forward.

HIRAM

(continuing)

I presume you're the 13th McConkie. Allow me to extend my sympathies on your unfortunate accident.

The ghost continues to come forward and takes a lethal swipe at Hiram with the mace. Hiram ducks under the blow, and springs to the wall where some weapons are hanging. He takes down a heavy claymore and springs to face the ghost, who is putting on the helmet. Now being able to see, the ghost is much more mobile and he goes after Hiram. A conflict then rages around the room, back and forth across the prostrate and unconscious form of Prentice. Hiram parries and slashes with his claymore in the manner of one born to the Highlands and the ghost gradually is forced onto the defensive. Eventually, simultaneous swings of both weapons result in the mace being cut off short at the handle and the ghost, finding himself weaponless, falls on his knees in the traditional attitude of submission. He speaks for the first time.

EARL

I yield! Mercy, your highness! I yield!

TWO SHOT - HIRAM AND EARL

Hiram steps forward and takes the helmet from the head of his foe, exposing the face of the Earl.

HIRAM

I hardly think this comes within the bounds of hospitality.

EARL

I was paid by your enemies, gracious monarch! Curse them! They called you a weakling king! Mercy!

HIRAM

I shall have to turn your case over to the proper court of law.

EARL

Rather the mercy of the hardest court than the blade of your claymore!

HIRAM

Why, thank you. Now, if you don't mind rising...

FULL SHOT-ROOM

As the Earl rises, the door bursts open and Ulrich comes in with several members of the Scottish constabulary. Ulrich points to the Earl.

ULRICH

Arrest the assassin!

As the constables come forward to take charge of the Earl, the Queen enters and flies to the side of Hiram.

QUEEN

Siegfried! You are not wounded? Had they harmed you, I should want to die!

HIRAM

That's very nice of you.

QUEEN

My bravest Siegfried!

Ulrich steps forward.

ULRICH

Madam...he is not your king.

QUEEN

What madness do you speak, Ulrich?

ULRICH

I speak the truth, madam.

He goes to the door and calls.

ULRICH

(continuing)

It is safe for you to enter, sire!

He steps back from the doorway, to await the entrance of someone outside.

FULL SHOT - GROUP

All eyes are turned wonderingly toward the door.

MED. CLOSE SHOT - AT DOOR

Siegfried the First makes his entrance. He glances around, then speaks.

SIEGFRIED

Hiram Holliday, you have done well.

FULL SHOT - ROOM

The Queen looks in amazement at Siegfried, then at Hiram.

QUEEN

You...are not Siegfried?

Hiram speaks with polite regret.

HIRAM

No.

> SIEGFRIED

Obviously he is not. A hireling was necessary to expose my enemies.

> QUEEN

> (to Siegfried)

You let him come here in your stead...in spite of the peril?

> SIEGFRIED

It was my patriotic duty to Rovakia. Come, madam.

> QUEEN

I shall come...it is also my patriotic duty. But first...

She crosses to Hiram.

TWO SHOT - HIRAM AND QUEEN

She kisses him on the cheek.

> QUEEN

> (continuing)

Hiram Holliday, I think you are the bravest man that I shall ever know. Adieu.

FULL SHOT - ROOM

The king offers the queen his arm and she goes out with the briefest of backward looks at Hiram.

> ULRICH

What happened here must remain forever secret. You will all understand that.

HIRAM

Oh, of course.

Ulrich motions the policeman out with the Earl and follows them out. Hiram bends down to revive Prentice.

TWO SHOT - HIRAM AND PRENTICE

HIRAM

Mr Prentice.

Prentice starts to revive.

WIDER ANGLE

Joel Smith rushes in as Prentice is reviving.

JOEL

Hiram! What's going on?

(sees Prentice)

What happened to him?

Prentice sits up.

PRENTICE

Where have you been, Smith? Why is it you always wander off when there's a story under your nose?

JOEL

What story? What happened here?

PRENTICE

Why, there was this...and then I...

(breaks off)

Holliday, you tell him!

HIRAM

I really regret not being able to tell you. But it's my patriotic duty.

He puts his hand to his cheek, gazing off, as Prentice and Joel stare at him, then at one another.

FADE OUT

THE END

The Adventure of the Sea Cucumber

This was the fifth script to be commissioned and indeed, the fifth episode to air, on 31 October 1956. It first ran on the BBC on 9 August 1960 and was repeated on 19 February the following year. It was produced and directed by Phil Rapp and written by him, John Kohn and Bernard Drew. The cast included Sebastian Cabot as Gemmel, Maria De Rosa as Natasha, Mark Dana as Nordstrom and Fred Cavens as Wang.

FADE IN:

EXT. AIRPORT - DAY – (STOCK) FULL SHOT

This should establish a rather small airport somewhere in Southeast Asia, such as Malaya.

DISSOLVE THROUGH:

FULL SHOT – WAITING ROOM – DAY

Hiram and Joel enter, dressed in white and carrying their suitcases. They go to the single attendant behind the counter. A few other passengers are in the waiting room, Chinese and East Asians.

                    JOEL

Checking in for the flight to Hong Kong.

He hands the attendant his ticket, as does Hiram.

                    HIRAM

We're together.

                    ATTENDANT

Flight 32?

He looks at the two Americans rather closely.

                    JOEL

It hasn't left?

                    ATTENDANT

In a few minutes, Mr…

                    (looks at tickets)

Mr Smith. And Mr Holliday.

He stamps them through, taking their bags.

ATTENDANT

(continuing)

Just have a seat, if you please.

Joel and Hiram walk to a bench. CAMERA MOVES IN on the clerk. He gives Hiram and Joel another close look.

TWO SHOT – HIRAM AND JOEL

Joel looks at his watch.

JOEL

In three hours, we should be in Hong Kong.

HIRAM

Say. We're seasoned travellers by now, Joel.

JOEL

Ever wish you were back in New York as a proof-reader, Hiram?

HIRAM

Not really. Do you? I mean, wish you were back, as a reporter?

JOEL

I could make it any day now, Hiram…if anything happens in Hong Kong, let me know, will you? Just let me know.

HIRAM

I just may have something for you, Joel. A long search that may come to an end. For Psolus ephippifer.

                              JOEL

                           (startled)

Who's he?

                             HIRAM

A rare form of sea-cucumber. It should make quite a scoop, don't you think?

Joel looks at him.

                              JOEL

I'll wire Prentice to hold the front page.

A voice comes over the PA with an announcement in Chinese, then makes the same announcement in English.

                               PA

Flight 32 for Hong Kong is now boarding at Gate Four. All aboard, please.

FULL SHOT – WAITING ROOM

Joel and Hiram rise, as do the other passengers.

                              JOEL

That's us, Hiram.

They go out, along with others in the waiting room. As they do, a blonde Scandinavian type comes in with his suitcase and goes to the counter.

                           NORDSTROM

Flight 32?

ATTENDANT

Now boarding. Your ticket?

Nordstrom gives him his ticket and bag. The clerk checks it.

ATTENDANT

Gate Four, Mr Nordstrom. A pleasant flight.

After a quick look around the waiting room, Nordstrom goes out. CAMERA MOVES IN on the attendant, who looks after Nordstrom with interest and satisfaction, then picks up the phone and dials the operator.

ATTENDANT

Hong Kong 4768...Hello? This is your friend. There are three Occidentals only on Flight 32.You should encounter no difficulty in picking out your man. None.

He puts down the phone, as we:

FADE OUT:

(FIRST COMMERCIAL)

FADE IN:

ESTABLISHING SHOT – HONG KONG – DAY (STOCK)

CLOSE SHOT – CAFÉ SIGN

A sign reads in both Chinese and English, "Café of the Seven Lotus Blossoms."

DISSOLVE THROUGH:

INT. CAFÉ – DAY – FULL SHOT

This is a cosmopolitan Hong Kong café. Overhead, a fan stirs the air slowly. Around the sides of the café are booths, sparsely populated. CAMERA PANS room to take in several sailors who are the only other customers, then MOVES IN on three people in a booth at some distance from the sailors. There is a large CHINESE, a rather dissolute sea CAPTAIN with a captain's hat pushed back on his head, and a striking-looking WOMAN who might be Russian. She is smoking a cigarette in a bored manner, and the three are waiting for a fourth member of the group. CAMERA PULLS BACK, and we see a large, almost obese man in a white suit and soft straw hat approaching the booth. His bearing denotes authority and purpose. This is GEMMEL. He sits down at the booth without any greeting to the others, and pulls from his inside coat pocket an envelope which he passes to the Captain.

MED SHOT – BOOTH

The captain opens the envelope, pulls out a large packet of bills, and leafs through them.

> GEMMEL

All there?

The captain nods, Gemmel continues.

> GEMMEL

> (continuing)

The plan is complete. Your junk will weigh anchor at twelve noon tomorrow, precisely.

> CAPTAIN

It's a ship, Gemmel.

Gemmel tosses off this old complaint.

GEMMEL

A ship that looks like a junk. There is just one more item.

CAPTAIN

What?

GEMMEL

You will be carrying a passenger.

CAPTAIN

No passengers.

GEMMEL ignores the captain.

GEMMEL

A passenger who will leave with you, but who will not arrive at your destination. Clear?

CAPTAIN

Murder was not in the bargain.

GEMMEL

No? You would rather he attached a little device to your junk which would have a disastrous effect on your…ah…rather explosive cargo?

NATASHA

Gemmel! The other side has found out about the arms?

GEMMEL

They have sent a man. My information is that he arrives this afternoon, on Flight 32. We will be there to meet him. You, Natasha, and you, Wang. Then we bring him to you, Captain.

NATASHA

You will know him, Gemmel?

Gemmel considers this slightly ridiculous.

GEMMEL

There are three Occidentals only on the plane. Out of them I cannot pick the Captain's future passenger?

NATASHA

Yes. But a mistake could cost us our lives.

GEMMEL

There will be no mistake. To your part you will bring your own rather obvious assets, and to my part I will contribute what I can. Brains. Success.

On the word "success" Gemmel raises his glass. The others follow suit.

DISSOLVE:

CLOSE SHOT – SIGN

The sign reads "Hong Kong Customs...Arriving Passengers." The legend is repeated in Chinese.

DISSOLVE THROUGH:

INT. CUSTOMS – FULL SHOT

The Customs Officer has just finished checking the baggage of Hiram and Nordstrom. He hands Hiram his bag, then Nordstrom.

MED. CLOSE SHOT - GROUP

Hiram takes his bag and puts it beside Joel's. Nordstrom puts his bag beside Hiram's, and it is apparent that the two bags closely resemble each other. CAMERA PANS TO Gemmel, Natasha and Wang, just entering the building. Gemmel looks in the direction of the three arrivals, and smiles with satisfaction.

MED. SHOT – GEMMEL'S POV

Hiram and Joel are looking around, as Nordstrom stands a little apart from them.

TWO SHOT – GEMMEL AND NATASHA

Gemmel points.

> GEMMEL

That one, Natasha.

He looks around to make sure they are not observed, as Natasha stares, puzzled.

> NATASHA

That one?

TWO SHOT – HIRAM AND NORDSTROM – NATASHA'S POV

Hiram has stepped over in front of Nordstrom, looking around.

TWO SHOT - GEMMEL AND NATASHA

Gemmel does not bother to look, in answer to her question. He is still making sure the coast is clear.

> GEMMEL

> (impatiently)

Of course. Go.

FULL SHOT – ROOM

Hiram is taken totally unaware as Natasha comes up to him, throws her arms around his neck and kisses him quite thoroughly.

NATASHA

Welcome to Hong Kong, my beloved!

Joel stares. Hiram is somewhat startled, but not displeased.

HIRAM

Thank you. I assume you were sent by the Chamber of Commerce.

ANOTHER ANGLE

Gemmel appears behind Hiram, giving Natasha a furious look and shaking his head violently. He then points to Nordstrom.

HIRAM

I should like to introduce my friend Joel Smith, who might also appreciate your…

Natasha freezes him.

NATASHA

How dare you???

She moves quickly to Nordstrom, and repeats the embrace.

NATASHA

(continuing)

Welcome, my beloved!

TWO SHOT – JOEL AND HIRAM

They stare, totally confused.

TWO SHORT – NORDSTROM AND NATASHA

As Nordstrom has his arms pinned by Natasha, Wang comes up behind him and pokes a gun in his back, so that it cannot be seen except from a very few feet away.

> WANG
> (low)

Pick up your suitcase and come with us, as if nothing had happened. Quick.

Nordstrom stiffens, taking in the situation. He looks at his suitcase.

CLOSE SHOT – SUITCASES

MED SHOT – GROUP

Nordstrom, instead of taking his own, reaches down and picks up Hiram's suitcase. The group moves off, Wang holding his gun very close, Natasha on Nordstrom's arm and smiling up at him, and Gemmel bringing up the rear. CAMERA MOVES WITH them to the door, then SWINGS BACK to Hiram and Joel.

> JOEL

What do you make of that?

> HIRAM

I believe we have reached the mysterious Orient.

> DISSOLVE:

CLOSE SHOT – CAFÉ SIGN – DAY

This is the Lotus Blossom sign.

> DISSOLVE THROUGH:

FULL SHOT – CAFÉ BACK ROOM – DAY

This is a small, sparsely furnished room. Gemmel listens at the door as Wang finishes gagging Nordstrom, who is bound to a chair. Gemmel turns from the door.

> GEMMEL

Take him in the other room.

Wang picks up Nordstrom, chair and all, and carries him through a door to an adjoining room. Gemmel turns to Natasha.

> GEMMEL

> (continuing)

Fool. Bungler.

> NATASHA

But Gemmel! You pointed to…

> GEMMEL

Enough. We have our man and we have our suitcase. No thanks to you.

He picks up the suitcase, and puts it on a chair. The Captain stirs nervously.

> CAPTAIN

Careful of that, Gemmel.

> GEMMEL

You would prefer to leave the room as I open it?

> CAPTAIN

I would, yes.

He starts off. Gemmel stops him with a word.

> GEMMEL

Stay where you are.

He goes over the bag with his fingers.

> GEMMEL

> (continuing)

I was not born yesterday, nor do I die today.

> (satisfied)

No hidden detonators. Now.

He starts to open the bag.

TWO SHOT – NATASHA AND THE CAPTAIN

They are staring in fright.

CLOSE SHOT – GEMMEL

His face reflects the strain as he slowly opens the bag. CAMERA PULLS BACK SLIGHTLY as he gets it open, and stares inside. The Captain and Natasha crowd in for a look. Gemmel takes something from the bag, and holds it up in amazement.

> GEMMEL

A butterfly net?

He picks up something else.

> GEMMEL

> (continuing)

A rock collection?

He dives in again.

GEMMEL

(continuing)

A stuffed bat?

He then drops what he has, and frantically begins to go through the bag, throwing articles of clothing out onto the floor.

GEMMEL

(continuing)

The explosives…where are the bombs??? Where are they???

Natasha gives a shrug.

NATASHA

Were it anyone else but Gemmel, I would say a mistake has been made.

Gemmel looks at her, then comes to a quick conclusion.

GEMMEL

Tricked. It was one of the two Americans. Our man is more clever than I had thought.

CAPTAIN

What do we do with your mistake?

He indicates the direction of the next room.

GEMMEL

Now, he knows too much. You will have two passengers, Captain.

(calling)

Wang!

(to Natasha)

We go to find the American.

INT. HOTEL ROOM – NIGHT – FULL SHOT

The room is furnished in Western style, except for a few Chinese touches. Joel is putting on his coat, preparatory to going out. The bathroom door is open, revealing Hiram at the mirror, shaving.

JOEL

Hurry it up, Hiram. I've got a great place for dinner...the Café of the Seven Lotus Blossoms.

HIRAM

Well, I am anxious to take up my quest for the sea cucumber.

JOEL

They might just serve them there.

CLOSE SHOT – HIRAM

HIRAM

I hardly think so Joel. Although the trepan is highly esteemed by the Chinese gourmet, the species Psolus Ephippifer of the sea cucumber is hardly ever found in...

(peers in mirror)

I believe I cut myself.

FULL SHOT – ROOM

JOEL

Never say ephippifer while shaving. Where's your styptic pencil?

HIRAM

In my bag, Joel. I'll keep my finger on the nearest pressure point.

JOEL

You do that.

MED. SHOT – JOEL

He picks up Hiram's suitcase and puts it on the bed, opening it.

CLOSE SHOT – JOEL

He reacts to the contents of the bag.

CLOSE SHOT – SUITCASE

In the suitcase can be seen a skindiver's outfit, including swim fins, and some rectangular objects which are magnetic bombs.

MED. CLOSE SHOT – JOEL

He holds up the swim fins, looking at them.

JOEL

Where'd you get the crazy slippers?

HIRAM

(o.s)

What?

JOEL

Never mind…where's the styptic pencil?

He has put back the fins and is looking through the bag.

HIRAM

(o.s)

In a little box, right on top.

Joel picks up one of the bombs, but can't figure out how to open it.

JOEL

I found the box, but how do you open it?

CLOSE SHOT – HIRAM

HIRAM

Just press the little button, Joel.

CLOSE SHOT – JOEL

He examines the bomb, pressing everything he can find.

JOEL

It seems to be stuck.

FULL SHOT – ROOM

Hiram comes in from the bathroom.

HIRAM

I sometimes have to shake it.

Joel shakes it violently, then listens. A TICKING SOUND is heard.

JOEL

It still won't open but I think I have it ticking.

(slight take)

Ticking?

CAMERA MOVES IN as Hiram comes closer.

HIRAM

I don't wish to alarm you, Joel, but you have just activated a bomb.

JOEL

Bomb??

He looks at it, horrified, not knowing what to do with it. Hiram takes it from his trembling grasp, and manipulates it so that the TICKING STOPS.

HIRAM

There. I disarmed it.

Joel sinks into a chair, terrified.

JOEL

Now…why are you carrying a thing like that in your suitcase?

Hiram looks into the suitcase.

HIRAM

I don't know…except that it doesn't seem to be my suitcase.

He reaches in, and pulls out another bomb.

HIRAM

(continuing)

See?...They're magnetized, so as to adhere to the hull of a ship.

He holds the two bombs close, and they come together with an audible 'clunk'. Joel is even more terrified.

JOEL

Hiram! Stop playing with them!

HIRAM

Oh, they're quite harmless...until activated.

Joel has by now risen and is backing off.

JOEL

Will you please put them away???

HIRAM

Developed by a British commando...the late A E Millhauser.

As he is speaking, he puts the bombs back in the suitcase. Joel rushes over and hastily closes the suitcase. Relieved, he turns to Hiram.

JOEL

What happened to Millhauser?

HIRAM

They never found him. Say...I must have received the wrong bag at the airport.

JOEL

Get dressed. This goes to the authorities...right now!

Hiram is mildly surprised at Joel.

> HIRAM

Even before you have dinner?

> JOEL

Yes! For once I'm on the trail of a story, and I'm going to get it!

CLOSE SHOT – HIRAM

He looks at Joel admiringly.

> HIRAM

I believe you will, Joel. Could I borrow a clean pair of socks?

QUICK DISSOLVE:

INT. HOTEL LOBBY – NIGHT – FULL SHOT

There are a few guests in the lobby, and a clerk behind the desk. CAMERA MOVES IN on Natasha, Gemmel and Wang seated in chairs where they can command a view of the lobby. They are closely observant, whilst pretending to be casual. Gemmel sees something over the top of his magazine, and slowly lowers it. He speaks to Natasha without turning.

> GEMMEL

There is our man. This time, no bungling.

Natasha also speaks without turning.

> NATASHA

I see him.

She rises and starts forward.

MED. SHOT – AT DESK

Hiram, carrying the suitcase, turns to the desk to give the key to the clerk. Joel walks on ahead. As he walks out of the scene, Natasha walks on.

NATASHA

Darling! Welcome to Hong Kong!

As Hiram puts down his suitcase, Natasha throws her arms around him, bending his back in a reverse Valentine, and kissing him.

TIGHT TWO SHOT – HIRAM AND NATASHA

Hiram looks up at her.

HIRAM

Well, thanks again.

She looks off, at Gemmel and Wang.

GEMMEL AND WANG – HER POV

Both have risen. Gemmel is shaking his head angrily, and gesturing in the direction of Joel.

MED. SHOT – AT DESK

The clerk is looking on in surprise as Natasha straightens up, releasing Hiram.

HIRAM

Perhaps by now I should introduce myself. My name is Hi –

Natasha freezes him again.

NATASHA

How dare you accost me, peasant??

HIRAM

But...

She goes off, in the direction of Joel, leaving Hiram and the clerk staring.

MED SHOT – JOEL

He is facing away from the action, so has not seen the exchange with Hiram. Natasha approaches him quickly from the side.

NATASHA

Darling! Welcome to Hong Kong!

She throws her arms around him, kissing him. Wang immediately moves in behind with his gun.

WANG

(low)

You will come with us, quietly.

Gemmel appears, speaking quietly to Wang and Natasha, without stopping.

GEMMEL

Take him away. I shall go and get the suitcase.

The trio of Wang, Joel and Natasha move off, with Natasha hanging on Joel's arm, smiling. CAMERA MOVES WITH them, then SWINGS BACK to Hiram at the desk.

HIRAM

(to clerk)

I don't really mind. You see, he's my best friend.

He somewhat wistfully picks up the suitcase and starts off.

DISSOLVE:

FULL SHOT – LOTUS BLOSSOM CAFÉ – NIGHT

CAMERA PANS café to swinging front doors as Hiram comes through them. He still has the suitcase with him, with his umbrella over the other arm. The beautiful Chinese CHECK GIRL approaches him from behind her counter.

MEI LAN

Welcome to the Café of the Seven Lotus Blossoms.

HIRAM

Thank you.

She takes the suitcase from him, and puts it in the check room, then turns to Hiram again.

MEI LAN

The gentleman is alone?

HIRAM

I am halfway expecting a friend…Mr. Joel Smith.

He gestures to indicate Joel's height.

HIRAM
(continuing)

American.

Mei Land shakes her head.

MEI LAN

Perhaps you will have a table while waiting for Mr. Smith.

                    HIRAM

Thank you.

She reaches for his umbrella, but he shakes his head.

                    HIRAM

                  (continuing)

I'll just carry it.

She hands him the check for the suitcase, and he goes off into the café proper.

FULL SHOT - CAFÉ BACK ROOM

Wang is going through the gag routine again, this time with Joel. Natasha and the Captain watch, as the door opens and Gemmel enters with Joel's suitcase. He takes in the scene quickly.

                   GEMMEL

Good. You were not followed here?

                   NATASHA

No.

                   GEMMEL

The other room, Wang.

Wang pushes the chair containing the bound and gagged Joel into the other room. The Captain looks after Joel doubtfully.

                   CAPTAIN

There will not be any more, Gemmel?

GEMMEL

(scornfully)

A few extra pounds might sink your staunch vessel.

CAPTAIN

(his one sore point)

Perhaps you can find a better one?

GEMMEL

If I had time, yes.

As he talks, he is putting the suitcase on a chair and starting to open it.

GEMMEL

(continuing)

Your craft is known throughout the Eastern Oceans as the Seagoing Cucumber. Ah.

He has the suitcase unlocked but does not open it.

GEMMEL

(continuing)

Natasha, your place is in the café. Go.

NATASHA

Of course, Gemmel.

She goes out. Gemmel mutters under his breath as she goes.

GEMMEL

Bungler.

MED. CLOSE SHOT – AT SUITCASE

Gemmel bends over it, in pleasurable but cautious anticipation. The Captain and Wang, who has come back from the other room, crowd in, looking on.

GEMMEL

Now.

As he lifts the lid, he speaks over his shoulder.

GEMMEL

(continuing)

I would not come too close.

The Captain and Wang draw back slightly. Gemmel slowly opens the suitcase all the way and peers inside.

CLOSE SHOT – GEMMEL

He registers puzzlement at what he sees. He reaches inside the suitcase and rummages around in it quickly.

GEMMEL

I don't understand.

CAPTAIN

(o.s)

Something gone wrong?

Gemmel starts pulling clothes out of the bag and flinging them around the room.

FULL SHOT – ROOM

Clothes are flying in all directions.

GEMMEL

Shirts! Ties! Underwear!

Wang takes the suitcase and holds it up, emptying out the rest of the contents.

WANG

Nothing.

Gemmel turns on him.

GEMMEL

You blundering idiot, again you have taken the wrong man!!

WANG

But…

GEMMEL

My entire life I must be surrounded by idiots!! Don't you see??

WANG

See what?

GEMMEL

All along it was the small one! The one with the glasses, the umbrella! Before he finds our ship, we must find him! Go!!

Wang and the Captain look at Gemmel, then start out as we:

FADE OUT:

End of Act One

Act Two

FADE IN:

FULL SHOT – NIGHT – CAFÉ

Hiram is seated at a booth in the café, eating a Chinese dish with chopsticks, which he handles with proficiency. A few feet away from the booth are some drapes, which apparently lead to the rear of the café. As Hiram is eating, the drapes part and Gemmel and Wang come through. They do not notice Hiram, nor does he notice them. They walk across the floor of the café, then Gemmel motions Wang to a halt.

TWO SHOT – GEMMEL and WANG

GEMMEL

(looking around)

Where is Natasha?

WANG

Perhaps drinking with a customer.

GEMMEL

Always when we need her, she...

(breaks off)

Look!

Wang follows his gaze.

CLOSE SHOT – HIRAM – THEIR POV

He is happily eating, unaware of their scrutiny...

TWO SHOT – WANG AND GEMMEL

GEMMEL

The small American. We look no further. Get Natasha.

WANG

She comes now.

FULL SHOT – CAFÉ

Natasha, in a skin tight gown, is slinking across the floor in a route which will take her by Hiram's booth.

MED SHOT – AT BOOTH

Hiram looks up and sees Natasha coming. He gets to his feet and turns his cheek as she comes into the picture.

HIRAM

I suppose you shall want to kiss me again.

Natasha, without stopping, slaps him full in the face and continues walking.

CLOSE SHOT – HIRAM

He stares after her, putting his hand up to his cheek.

HIRAM

I guess I don't understand women.

He gives his characteristic shrug, and sits down again.

MED. SHOT – OTHER SIDE OF ROOM

Gemmel and Wang have slipped in to a booth. As Natasha passes them, Gemmel grabs her wrist and quickly pulls her into the booth.

MED. CLOSE SHOT – BOOTH

GEMMEL

Fool! Dumkopf! All day you are kissing him, and now you slap him!

Natasha rubs her wrist.

NATASHA

Why not?

GEMMEL

Why not? Why not?? He is our man!

NATASHA

What happened to our other man?

GEMMEL

Never mind. This is the one. The small American.

NATASHA

But I thought…

GEMMEL

Let me do the thinking. You are to dance with him. Then, lead him to the portieres.

He nods his head in the direction of the drapes.

GEMMEL

(continuing)

Behind them, Wang will be waiting.

NATASHA

I understand.

GEMMEL

Take no chances. This is the most dangerous man in the Orient.

He looks in the direction of Hiram. Hiram also looks.

HIRAM – THEIR POV

He is eating with his chopsticks, looking not at all dangerous.

AT BOOTH

Natasha addresses Gemmel. Still looking towards Hiram.

NATASHA

Gemmel…are you sure this is the man?

GEMMEL

Go!

She rises, and starts across towards Hiram.

MED. SHOT – HIRAM'S BOOTH

Hiram looks up as Natasha comes INTO PICTURE, and stops in front of his booth.

NATASHA

Natasha has returned.

HIRAM

Pardon my seeming churlishness, but what does Natasha have in mind?

NATASHA

You.

HIRAM

Oh. Well, won't you sit down?

He indicates the space opposite him, and continues talking.

HIRAM

(continuing)

I did want to ask you about Joel Smith, the tall American who...

Instead of sitting opposite him, Natasha sits next to him, forcing him over. Hiram continues speaking, but is slightly crowded as he gestures towards Joel's height.

HIRAM

(continuing)

...the tall American who left the hotel with you.

NATASHA

He did not appeal to me. I dropped him.

HIRAM

I see. Do you happen to remember where?

NATASHA

No. I am concerned only with you.

HIRAM

Really?

> NATASHA

I want to know all about you.

> HIRAM

That's very flattering, but I've never known Joel to wander off like this, and I...

> NATASHA

What do you do in Hong Kong, my small American?

> HIRAM

Actually I'm here searching for a certain sea cucumber.

> NATASHA

Ah. Then I shall help you.

> HIRAM

I didn't think you'd be interested in things like that.

She glances towards the portieres.

PORTIERES – POV

There is a slight movement behind them.

AT BOOTH

Natasha looks back at Hiram.

> NATASHA

But first, we dance.

> HIRAM

Thank you, but I feel I should look for my friend.

She rises, and pulls him up imperiously.

NATASHA

We dance!

HIRAM

Of course.

She puts her arm around him, and they dance onto the floor.

FULL SHOT – CAFÉ

There are several other couples dancing as Hiram and Natasha glide onto the floor. Hiram is concentrating seriously on his steps, while Natasha is trying to steer him over to the drapes.

CLOSE SHOT – BEHIND DRAPES

Wang sneeks a peak, then drops the curtain and waits, with a heavy mallet poised.

MED SHOT – DANCE FLOOR

Natasha has Hiram close to the drapes, and his head comes very near being in position.

CLOSE SHOT – WANG

He starts to swing his mallet.

MED SHOT – DANCE FLOOR

With a fancy step, Hiram dances away from the drapes, and a nearby couple dance into the position occupied seconds before by Hiram and Natasha. The man weaves dizzily, then slowly collapses on the floor. This business is repeated several times, INTERCUTTING to Wang peering through the drapes, and then swinging his mallet, and CUTTING TO REACTION SHOTS of Natasha, who just can't put Hiram on the spot. Hiram himself is dancing up a storm, unaware of what is going on. Finally, the MUSIC STOPS.

TWO SHOT – HIRAM AND NATASHA

Hiram claps politely.

HIRAM

Say, that was fun.

He looks around. CAMERA PANS dance floor, littered with bodies, then SWINGS BACK to Hiram and Natasha.

HIRAM

(continuing)

The classic symptoms are those of a typhus outbreak.

NATASHA

It is nothing. The patrons drink too much. Come…I want to be alone with you.

She takes his hand, but Hiram resists.

HIRAM

This time, I must refuse. I believe the police should be notified about Joel.

NATASHA

I have just remembered. I can take you to him. This way.

FULL SHOT – CAFÉ

She leads him by the hand towards the portieres, but as they go Hiram picks up his umbrella from the booth where he has been sitting. As they go through the drapes, CAMERA HOLDS for a moment on the carnage on the floor, with the women reviving their escorts.

MED. CLOSE SHOT – BACK HALL

Natasha and Hiram come down from the dimly lit back hall and stop in front of a door.

                    NATASHA

Your friend is in there.

                    HIRAM

I'm not sure that I entirely believe you.

                    NATASHA

If you wish to join him, enter.

HIRAM looks at her, then opens the door and goes in. She follows him.

REVERSE SHOT – AT DOOR

Hiram comes through the door, and then reacts slightly to what he sees.

ROOM – HIRAM'S POV

Wang is standing, holding a murderous looking curved sword. Gemmel rises from a chair, opening a large switch-blade knife.

                    GEMMEL

Come in, come in.

ROOM – ANOTHER ANGLE

Hiram enters, as Natasha closes the door behind him.

                    GEMMEL

               (continuing; to Natasha)

Search him!

NATASHA

I have…as we danced.

Hiram gives her a look

GEMMEL

And he carries no weapon. A bold man.

HIRAM

Thank you.

GEMMEL

And where is your suitcase, my dear fellow?

HIRAM

I should like very much to know. I shall need a chance of socks.

GEMMEL

I doubt that you will.

Wang advances menacingly.

WANG

The suitcase, American!

GEMMEL

It makes no difference. This one will get no chance to use the bombs.

WANG

I shall bind and gag him?

GEMMEL

No. He is too dangerous to treat as we have done the others. For him, the end will come more swiftly.

Gemmel has his knife in readiness.

HIRAM

One question. You do have my friend Joel Smith?

GEMMEL

He sails tomorrow, at noon. On a ship whose cargo will ignite the powder keg of the Orient...but your friend I not completing the journey. Wang!

At the command, Wang comes forward with his sword, and Gemmel with his knife. As they lunge at Hiram, he parries their blows with his umbrella. Wang starts taking vicious swings at Hiram, as if he were swinging a baseball bat. Hiram dodges one, then hooks his umbrella on an overhead rafter just in time to pull himself up, out of the way of the next swing. Gemmel and Wang both converge on him, and Hiram—hanging from the rafter—kicks out with his feet, knocking them both over. Hiram runs to the door, as Natasha shrinks to one side.

HIRAM

Excuse me.

He dashes out the door, as Gemmel and Wang get to their feet and come after him.

FULL SHOT – CAFÉ

The café is just getting back to normal again, when Hiram bursts through the portieres, and turns to face his adversaries as they come after him. He retreats across the dance floor toward the front entrance, parrying their blows as he goes. CAMERA TRAVELS with the battle. Near the front entrance and checkroom, Hiram gains a little time by knocking over a table in the path of Gemmel and Wang.

ANOTHER ANGLE – AT CHECK COUNTER

As Mei Lan stares, Hiram quickly pulls out his check and gives it to her. Before she has time to hand him the suitcase, Gemmel and Wang are on him again, and the fight rages back into the café. As they come back past the checkroom again, Mei hands Hiram the suitcase. He takes it, and fights his adversaries back into the café. Mei Lan stares after him. Hiram then reappears, gains a little more time by tipping over another table, and in a fast move hands Mei Lan his umbrella while he reaches in his pocket. Bringing out a coin, he gives it to her, and takes his umbrella just as Gemmel and Wang are on him again. With a quick thrust which forces them back, Hiram then makes a dash out the front doors. As they follow they are met by the two swinging doors, and bowled over. As they lie prostrate, Natasha comes on the scene, staring.

DISSOLVE:

JUNK – DAY – FULL SHOT (STOCK)

This is a Chinese junk riding at anchor…preferably a junk that resembles a sea-going cucumber.

SECTION OF DECK – DAY – MED. CLOSE SHOT.

Joel and Nordstrom are lying side by side, tied up and leaning against a hatch. Nordstrom squints up at the sky.

NORDSTROM

Dawn. Soon they will come back, and things will happen.

JOEL

We've still got a chance.

NORDSTROM

What chance? My friend, this is the most dangerous ship that sails the seas. If its cargo reaches its destination…

JOEL

I know.

NORDSTROM

I was the one man who could have stopped it. I failed, and we both pay with our lives. And we are only the first.

JOEL

I say we've got a chance. Hiram Holliday has the bombs.

Nordstrom takes no encouragement from this.

NORDSTROM

He is a demolition expert? A frogman who can swim out in Hong Kong harbour without being seen? A bird dog who can smell out this ship above all others?

JOEL

He not only can, he will. And he'll blow this ship five thousand miles high!

NORDSTROM
(quietly)

For us, that is a chance?

JOEL stares at him, stricken by the realisation.

CLOSE SHOT – HIRAM

He is in the water, in his frogman's outfit. He peers ahead, then does a flip-over and dives beneath the surface.

UNDERWATER SHOT

Hiram is swimming underwater, kicking along with his fins.

ANOTHER ANGLE – UNDERWATER

The hull of the junk looms ahead. Hiram swims up to the hull, and removes a bomb from his belt, attaching it to the hull with a loud and metallic CLANK. He takes another bomb and attaches it a few feet from the first, with another CLANK.

MED. CLOSE SHOT – JOEL AND NORDSTROM

Nordstrom reacts to a loud CLANK.

                    NORDSTROM

   Listen!

                    JOEL

   What is it?

There is another CLANK.

                    NORDSTROM

   You hear it?

                    JOEL

   Yes. What…?

                    NORDSTROM

   There is only one sound in the world like that. Your friend is attaching his bombs to the hull of the ship.

There is another CLANK.

JOEL

(yells)

Hiram!

MED. SHOT – UNDERWATER

Hiram attaches another bomb to the hull, with the usual CLANK.

MED. SHOT – JOEL AND NORDSTROM

NORDSTROM

He can't hear you. And those are set to go off in five minutes.

JOEL

What are we going to do?

NORDSTROM

I'll take my chances in the water.

He starts to roll himself to the edge of the deck.

JOEL

But how can I swim with my hands and feet tied?

NORDSTROM

Perhaps you had better learn.

He rolls off the edge and Joel starts to follow.

MED. SHOT – UNDERWATER

Hiram has attached what he believes to be the last of his bombs to the hull, and turns to go when Joel comes past him, trailing bubbles on his way down. Joel frantically opens his mouth in a cry for help, but all he accomplishes is to swallow more water. Hiram starts after him, but is brought back against the hull by some unseen force. He pushes off again, with more urgency, and is brought back again. After this is repeated once more, Hiram feels around the back of his belt, and finds one of the magnetic bombs still hooked there. He hastily detaches it, and puts it against the hull. He then swims off after Joel.

BEACH – DAY – MED. SHOT

Joel is stretched out on the beach. Hiram is astride Joel, giving him artificial respiration. Nordstrom, unbound, is looking expectantly out to sea. There is a LOUD EXPLOSION, and Hiram turns to look.

LONG VIEW – MASSIVE EXPLOSION (STOCK)

This is the grand-daddy of all explosions, combined with a sustained display of pyrotechnics.

MED. SHOT – BEACH

Hiram and Nordstrom turn to look at each other, awed. Nordstrom extends his hand.

NORDSTROM

You have preserved the peace of the world.

Joel raises his head, and Hiram gets off to allow him to sit up.

JOEL

What…what happened?

NORDSTROM

Nothing. Not a word of this must ever reach print.

JOEL

Why?? It's the best story of my career and I uncovered it.

NORDSTROM

The diplomatic consequences, my friend, might be far more serious than that explosion. Not a word.

He looks out to sea again.

JOEL

Hiram! I can't print it!

HIRAM

Don't worry Joel. You found the Psolus Ephippifer

JOEL

What?

HIRAM

Look. A rare sea cucumber.

He extracts a sea cucumber from Joel's breast pocket, as Joel stares.

FADE OUT:

FADE IN:

INT. HOTEL ROOM – DAY – FULL SHOT

Joel is shaving, with the bathroom door open, as Hiram is admiring his specimen of sea cucumber. Joel is struck by a sudden thought and comes to the door of the bathroom.

JOEL

Hiram.

HIRAM

What, Joel?

JOEL

I just realised…you know with all the excitement I haven't eaten since we got to Hong Kong.

HIRAM

Say, that's right. I can recommend the cuisine at the Café of the Seven Lotus Blossoms.

JOEL

I'd just as soon go some other place.

HIRAM

But the British authorities took care of Gemmel and his employees.

JOEL

Just the same…

HIRAM

As you say, Joel.

JOEL

I could eat a horse.

HIRAM

You know, this little fellow has an interesting method of eating.

JOEL

Psolus Ephippifer?

HIRAM

Oh, you know him. Well, he casts out his visceral organs, including his stomach, into the surrounding ocean. Then, when he has thus entangled an enemy, he grows a new stomach, the prey meanwhile being held by the old, after which ingestion sets in, and Psolus enjoys a hearty meal. Well, shall we eat?

                    JOEL

                (a little green)

I think I'll wait a while.

He goes back into the bathroom, as Hiram speaks DIRECTLY INTO CAMERA

                   HIRAM

Sometimes I don't understand him at all.

FADE OUT:

                  The End.

But it wasn't just Joel's stomach that was turned by the sea cucumber's antics. That final scene was revised on 14th August 1956:

FADE IN:

INT. HOTEL ROOM – DAY – FULL SHOT

Hiram is seated, admiring his sea cucumber, while Joel is staring straight ahead, still brooding.

JOEL

I can't get over it…the biggest story of the year…of the decade…and I can't print a word of it.

HIRAM

Oh, well.

JOEL

"Oh well?" Is that all you can say, Hiram?

HIRAM

Perhaps it's all for the best.

JOEL

(getting hot)

"Perhaps it's all for the best?" An international ring of gun-runners rounded up, an explosion that rocks Hong Kong… Prentice is back home screaming for copy and I can't send him a word??

HIRAM

While I do not favour suppression of the news, in this case we should both be duly grateful.

JOEL

Grateful? Why??

HIRAM

I just got a copy of the local fish and game rules. We have captured Psolus Ephippifer entirely out of season.

As Hiram looks at the sea cucumber, Joel stares at Hiram. CAMERA PANS to CLOSE SHOT of Joel, who speaks INTO CAMERA.

JOEL

Sometimes I don't understand him at all.

CAMERA PANS BACK to Hiram as we:

FADE OUT:

The End.

The Adventure of the Hawaiian Hamzah

This was the tenth script that was commissioned but the eighth episode to be aired. NBC broadcast it on 21 November 1956 whilst the BBC ran it on 19 August 1960 and again on 12 March the following year. It was produced, written and directed by Philip Rapp. Sometime between script and production Sebastian Cabot became unavailable to film so the character of Gemmel was changed to Kovatch and played by John Wengraf.. Other cast members included Lei Aloha as Moana and Albert Cavens as Andre.

FADE IN:

EXT. WAIKIKI BEACH-DAY- STOCK - ESTABLISHING SHOT MONTAGE

These should be the standard shots of the surfers, the out rigger canoes riding the waves, and the sunbathers on the beach, winding up with a view of the Royal Hawaiian or whatever plush hotel is available.

DISSOLVE THROUGH:

INT. LANAI – DAY - FULL SHOT

This should simulate the Royal Hawaiian Lanai and Surf Bar. A number of guests are lounging in beach clothing. CAMERA MOVES IN on JOEL and HIRAM. Joel is very much at his ease, in a loud Aloha shirt and shorts, and sipping from a very tall drink. Hiram is in his usual suit, intensely absorbed in a book.

HIRAM

Say! This is interesting.

JOEL

Mm?

HIRAM

The Hawaiian equivalent, Joel, of our word "across" can only be stated thusly...mai kekahi oaoa a I kekahi aoao ae.

JOEL

Oh.

HIRAM

I find him a most stimulating author.

JOEL

Who, Hiram?

HIRAM

(holding up the book)

Professor Henry P. Codd, the definitive authority on the language of the islands.

JOEL

Oh.

HIRAM

He is most helpful in my search for the elusive hamzah.

Joel almost sits up.

JOEL

Hamzah?

HIRAM

A language sign representing the Hawaiian lost consonant... first cousin to a "k", the authorities believe.

JOEL

Lost consonant?

HIRAM

It is written so...

(he writes in the air)

...as an inverted and reversed apostrophe.

JOEL

(sitting up heavily)

Hiram. We've been a week in beautiful Hawaii...matchless playground paradise of the Pacific. And what have you done for the whole week?...Read Henry P. Codd and look for hamzahs.

HIRAM

But, Joel...without the lost consonant, expressed as a glottal stop, the ancient Hawaiian chants would lack not only charm, but authenticity.

JOEL

Forget the glottal stops! Look around! Live a little!

A beautiful girl in a scant swimsuit passes in front of Joel, and he interrupts his speech to follow her progress.

JOEL

(continuing; resuming)

Uh... live a little.

HIRAM

(rising)

Excellent advice, Joel. I shall follow it.

JOEL

Where are you going?

HIRAM

To have lunch with Professor Codd. Poi and baked hamzah, I believe.

He laughs up his little joke, and goes off.

CLOSE SHOT - JOEL

He stares after Hiram, then shrugs and picks up his drink.

PRENTICE (o.s.)

Smith!

Joel chokes on his drink, spinning around.

TWO SHOT - PRENTICE AND JOEL

PRENTICE is staring disapprovingly at Joel, who scrambles to his feet.

JOEL

Mr. Prentice! I thought you were in New York!

Prentice looks him up and down.

PRENTICE

I can see you did. Where's Hiram Holliday?

JOEL

He just this minute left, Mr. Prentice.

PRENTICE

It's not your job to go with him, wherever he goes?

SMITH

Well, he's off looking for lost consonants...hamzahs.

PRENTICE

Hamzahs??

He takes the tall drink out of Joel's hand, sniffs it and passes it back.

PRENTICE

(continuing)

I see.

JOEL

Actually.

PRENTICE

Yes. Now, you listen to me, Smith.

JOEL

Yes, Mr. Prentice.

PRENTICE

I can see what's been going on here...on my money. But that's not the reason I'm here.

Joel brightens slightly.

JOEL

No?

PRENTICE

No. There's a story here in Hawaii...the signing of the Pacific Mutual Assistance Pact at Pearl Harbor tomorrow. We need a capable man to cover it.

JOEL

(all smiles)

I'll do my best, Mr. Prentice.

PRENTICE

We need a capable man to cover it, so I'm doing it myself. You are taking the plane at midnight, back to the States!

JOEL

Back to the States?

PRENTICE

Yes! Your travels are over, Smith! Oh, I'm not blaming you... it was my mistake.

JOEL

Well...

PRENTICE

(going right on)

I assigned you to get the story of Hiram Holliday because I thought you were hard-working; sober. But I was wrong! You've turned into a lotus-eater!

JOEL

But, Mr Prentice...

PRENTICE

Stories?? I haven't seen anything but bar bills and restaurant checks from every corner of the globe! Back to the States, Smith! Hamzahs indeed. Back to work!!

FADE OUT:

FIRST COMMERCIAL

FADE IN:

EXT. ROYAL HAWAIIAN - DAY - (STOCK) - FULL SHOT

DISSOLVE THRU:

INT. HOTEL LOBBY-DAY-FULL SHOT

Joel, dressed for travel, is waiting in line at the desk to check out. His bags are near him. Hiram enters and is about to go to the desk for his key when he sees Joel.

                    HIRAM

Oh, hello, Joel.

                    JOEL
                    (down)

Hello, Hiram.

                    HIRAM

I had a most exciting lunch with Professor Codd...you should have been there.

                    JOEL

I should have been.

Hiram looks more closely at the line in which Joel is standing.

                    HIRAM

I believe that you are in the wrong line...these people are checking out.

                    JOEL

So am I. Prentice is here. He's sending me back to the States.

HIRAM

Oh, really? Then I'd better go pack.

Joel stops him.

JOEL

Not you, Hiram. Just me. He says I've turned into a lotus-eater.

HIRAM

But he can't break up the old team, Joel. Perhaps if I talked to him...?

JOEL

Save your breath. Anyway, he's off covering the treaty-signing that takes place tomorrow.

HIRAM

Joel, I find this most distressing. I...

As Hiram is talking, he is bumped slightly by a portly man with a beard, going by him on the way to the desk. It is GEMMEL, rather thinly disguised with an eye-patch. He is accompanied by an exotic Polynesian girl and a strapping Hawaiian man. Hiram turns, seeing only the back of Gemmel.

TWO SHOT - HIRAM AND JOEL

Hiram stares after Gemmel.

HIRAM

(continuing)

Does that man look familiar to you, Joel?

Joel looks.

AT DESK - JOEL'S POV

Gemmel is making an inquiry of the clerk.

TWO SHOT - JOEL AND HIRAM

JOEL

Not particularly, no.

Hiram is still looking.

HIRAM

I'm sure I've seen him somewhere. Istanbul? Smolensk?

Joel puts a hand on Hiram's shoulder.

JOEL

Hiram...relax. My plane leaves at midnight...let's just enjoy ourselves till then. I've covered my last adventure of Hiram Holliday.

Hiram turns to him.

HIRAM

Joel. Stuff and nonsense.

QUICK DISSOLVE

INT. HOTEL CORRIDOR-DAY-FULL SHOT

It is a minute or two later, in a corridor of the same hotel. Gemmel and his two companions have paused outside the door of a hotel room. Gemmel is about to knock, when he sees someone coming down the corridor. He waits until the man, a small Asiatic, passes by. He watches him down the hall, then knocks...evidently a prearranged signal.

MED. CLOSE SHOT-AT DOOR

The door opens and a thin, almost gaunt MAN looks out. He stares at them silently, then without a word, steps back from the door to let them in. They enter.

INT. HOTEL ROOM-FULL SHOT

As they enter the room, Gemmel signals with a nod of the head for the Hawaiian, KEOKI, to remain by the door. He speaks to the girl.

GEMMEL

Moana.

He indicates for her to go to the window, and keep watch. Gemmel then sits, and turns to the thin man.

GEMMEL

(continuing)

Now.

The thin man stands looking at him, very nervous and in evident fear.

THIN MAN

You were not followed, Gemmel?

GEMMEL

I am not a child. I was not followed. You have it?

THIN MAN

I have it.

He hesitates.

GEMMEL

(impatiently)

Well?

The man turns, goes to the wall and takes down a picture, disclosing a wall safe.

CLOSE SHOT - AT SAFE

The thin man works the combination, opens the safe and takes out a small box. He closes the safe, replaces the picture, and turns back to Gemmel.

FULL SHOT - ROOM

Without a word, the thin man hands the box to Gemmel.

CLOSE SHOT - GEMMEL

He tears at the wrappings feverishly, his eyes shining...Sidney Greenstreet unwrapping the Maltese Falcon. He opens the long, thin box and takes out a pen, about a foot long and elaborately carved.

GEMMEL

Yes. That is all. That is all, and it makes the H-bomb as obsolete as the longbow.

MOANA

That?

GEMMEL

That. Climatic warfare, my dear Moana. As the H-bomb sets the air afire, this reacts with the water of the sea...turning it on contact into solid ice. I have simplified it for your mind, but that is the principle...the beautiful, deadly principle.

THIN MAN

I think you had better go.

GEMMEL

We shall go...in our own time. First, the test.

THIN MAN

Take my word, Gemmel, it...

Gemmel cuts him off.

GEMMEL

Moana. A glass of water. Now.

Moana goes off, into the bathroom. The thin man is more and more nervous.

THIN MAN

Every minute you are here with me, Gemmel...

GEMMEL

Quiet.

Moana re-enters with a glass of water. She gives it to Gemmel, who places it on a small table beside his chair.

CLOSE SHOT - GEMMEL

His eyes are shining with anticipation and excitement as he takes the cap off the pen.

GEMMEL

(continuing)

Ah. Now. Now.

Delicately, he brings the point of the pen in bare contact with the surface of the water.

CLOSE SHOT - GLASS

There is the SOUND of a crack as the glass breaks apart. It falls away from the solid ice inside the glass.

CLOSE SHOT - GEMMEL

He picks up the cylinder of ice.

GEMMEL

(continuing)

Yes. Yes!

FULL SHOT - ROOM

Laughing hugely, Gemmel tosses the cylinder of ice to Keoki at the door, then turns to the thin man.

GEMMEL

You have done well! Moana gives it to the American envoy tonight at the luau! Tomorrow, he signs the treaty on board ship and hurls the pen into the sea...transforming all Pearl Harbor into solid ice, and imprisoning the entire American fleet!!!

Again he bursts into huge laughter, as we:

DISSOLVE:

INT. RESTAURANT-NIGHT-FULL SHOT

This is a restaurant and nightclub where a luau is in progress. CAMERA MOVES IN on Joel and Hiram, seated at a table, eating.

> JOEL

> (bitterly)

Look at him, Hiram.

> HIRAM

Who, Joel?

> JOEL

Prentice. Stuffing his fat face.

Hiram turns and looks.

FULL SHOT - ANOTHER TABLE-HIRAM'S POV

Prentice is seated at a table groaning with food. With him is the President's personal envoy, a distinguished and slightly fatuous diplomat, along with several admirals and a general.

TWO SHOT - JOEL AND HIRAM

Joel continues to chew bitterly.

> JOEL

Came to Hawaii to cover the treaty signing, he says. He came here to eat!

> HIRAM

Joel. I should not let bitter thoughts of Mr. Prentice spoil our final evening.

> JOEL

You're right, Hiram. Pass the lomi lomi.

Hiram does so, and Joel digs in. Chewing, he casts another baleful look in the direction of Prentice.

JOEL

(continuing)

Look at him. Apple polisher!

FULL SHOT - PRENTICE'S TABLE

Prentice is buttering up the diplomat, DONN CHESTER DAVIES.

PRENTICE

How did you leave things in Washington, Mr. Davies?

DAVIES

All quiet on the Hill, Prentice. The Chief, of course, is depending on this treaty to ease things in the Pacific.

PRENTICE

Well, you and the administration have the full backing of my paper. I'm covering the signing myself, you know.

DAVIES

Should be a good show. I believe they're giving me a ceremonial pen tonight.

PRENTICE

Is there...ah...any truth to the rumors that a foreign power might try to block the signing?

DAVIES

(condescending)

I think, Prentice, that our people will take the necessary precautions.

PRENTICE

Of course, Mr. Davies. Of course.

CAMERA PANS from Prentice and Davies to a nearby table, STOP-PING on a CLOSE SHOT of the small Asiatic we saw in the hotel corridor. He is staring intently at Davies. CAMERA MOVES ON to drape which screens off an exit from the room.

CLOSE SHOT - AT DRAPE

A corner of the drape is slowly pulled back, and Gemmel peers out. Since he has forgotten that he is wearing his disguise, he has to raise his eye-patch to see. He looks around, then drops the curtain.

MED. CLOSE SHOT - BEHIND CURTAIN

Gemmel is there with Keoki and Moana. Both are made up to go on as entertainers...Keoki stripped to the waist and carrying a large ceremonial sword, and Moana dressed for a hula.

MOANA

They are there, Gemmel?

GEMMEL

The fatuous American, Davies...and his party. You know your part?

MOANA

Of course.

GEMMEL

Keoki?

KEOKI

The pen?

GEMMEL

When the time comes...not sooner.

MOANA

Gemmel...I have heard things.

GEMMEL

What things?

MOANA

That there is a man, who would block us. He is said to seek the weapon for his country.

GEMMEL

There is only one man I fear, and he is far away. Hiram Holliday. Any other I will deal with.

He suddenly has a small gun in his hand, as the others look down. He peeks out, then drops the curtain.

GEMMEL

(continuing)

It is time.

FULL SHOT - DANCE FLOOR

A host and MASTER OF CEREMONIES in a dinner jacket has pulled a microphone to the middle of the floor. He holds up his hands for silence.

MC

Welcome, welcome, welcome, friends and our distinguished guests, to the Pearl of the Pacific, to the House of Kamehameha, and to the luau of the ancient kings. Because no luau is complete without the hula, and no hula without its own story, we bring you Moana...telling with her hands and body a story for just this occasion. Moana.

He takes his microphone to one side as Moana enters and makes her bow to the audience.

TWO SHOT - HIRAM AND JOEL

> HIRAM

Isn't it about time to leave, Joel?

> JOEL

> (chewing and looking)

I've got time.

> HIRAM

I suppose you know best.

He turns his attention to Moana.

MED. SHOT - DANCE FLOOR

As the MUSIC STARTS, the MC, to one side with the mike, tells the story of the hula, as danced by Moana. The dance is INTER-CUT WITH SHOTS of Prentice and Davies, looking on with interest, Hiram and Joel, and of the small Asiatic, very tense and getting ready for a desperate move.

> MC

Far from the east we have come in our long canoes...in friendship, in peace, in love. Many days we have travelled, to meet with our haole brothers, the great chiefs of the west.

From the sea, we bring the writing stick which shall speak but once in friendship, in peace, in love...and then return to the god of the sea.

As Moana finishes her dance, she bows, and Keoki enters, carrying on the flat of his sword the box containing the pen. Davies rises and starts forward for the presentation.

CLOSE SHOT - THE ASIATIC

He rises and goes off swiftly, with evident purpose.

CLOSE SHOT - AT DRAPE

Gemmel, peering out, has seen the move and stands with his gun ready.

FULL SHOT - DANCE FLOOR

Moana takes the box from the sword of Keoki, opens it, and gives the pen with a bow to Davies.

CLOSE SHOT - AT SWITCHBOARD

The small Asiatic comes quickly into the picture, opens the switch box and pulls the main switch. The LIGHTS GO OUT.

A SCREAM is HEARD, there is the SOUND of running and confusion, the sudden FLASH of a gun and three or four SHOTS. The LIGHTS COME UP.

FULL SHOT - RESTAURANT

The scene is one of confusion. Davies, standing, looks around to see what has happened to the pen. Gemmel, caught in the open with his gun out, hastily conceals it and signals furiously to Keoki before disappearing behind the drape. Keoki starts forward.

MED. SHOT - HIRAM'S TABLE

Hiram and Joel are looking down.

CLOSE SHOT - ON FLOOR

The small Asiatic is sprawled by the table, face down.

MED. SHOT - HIRAM'S TABLE

JOEL

Hiram. That man's been shot!

HIRAM

(looking down)

I believe you're right, Joel. He also appears to have dropped something.

Hiram bends over and picks up the pen from the floor. Keoki comes into the scene, swiftly picks up the dead man and throws him over his shoulder like a sack of grain, and starts off with him.

FULL SHOT - DANCE FLOOR

The shaken MC takes the mike to the center of the floor, trying to carry on in the Hawaiian spirit.

MC

Our apologies, malahini and kamaaina, for the anger of the thunder god, who seems to have struck a light pole. But in happy islands, gaiety soon follows the storm, and now we...

He is forced to break off and duck the dangling legs of the stricken Asiatic as Keoki carries him swiftly by. The MC takes one startled glance after Keoki and his burden and finishes off on a doubtful not.

MC

(continuing)

...we shall have music?

An unseen band strikes up a LIVELY HAWAIIAN PIECE. Davies, still vastly puzzled, returns to his table.

CLOSE SHOT - HIRAM'S TABLE

Hiram is examining the pen with interest.

JOEL

What's going on here, Hiram? Why was he trying to get the pen? Why was he killed?

HIRAM

I don't know, Joel. But the writing stick apparently does not carry a lifetime guarantee.

MED. CLOSE SHOT - BEHIND DRAPE

Keoki is straightening up from searching the body of the small Asiatic.

KEOKI

He does not carry the pen.

GEMMEL

He must have it!! Where is it?? Who...?

He whips back a corner of the drape and peers out.

FULL SHOT – RESTAURANT - GEMMEL'S POV

Hiram has turned and is looking around the room.

MED. CLOSE SHOT - BEHIND DRAPE

Gemmel drops the drape, his face dark with fury.

GEMMEL

Holliday!! He is here!! He has the pen!!

MOANA

Hiram Holliday?

GEMMEL

Yes! It is his fine hand...I should have known. Moana! Get him. The small American with the glasses.

MOANA

He will come?

GEMMEL

He has an Achilles heel...women. Get him.

Moana lifts the drape and goes through.

CLOSE SHOT - HIRAM AND JOEL

JOEL

Look, Hiram. I think we ought to get out of here and go to the police.

HIRAM

But then you'd miss your plane.

JOEL

Forget the plane! There's been a murder here, and...

He breaks off, as he sees Hiram's attention is elsewhere.

                    JOEL

                  (continuing)

What's the matter?

                    HIRAM

I believe I am being paged.

Joel swivels around to look.

FULL SHOT – MOANA - THEIR POV

She is beckoning to Hiram.

MED. CLOSE SHOT- HIRAM'S TABLE

Hiram starts to rise, putting the pen in his coat pocket.

                    JOEL

Where are you going? It may be a trap!

                    HIRAM

You may be right, Joel. I'd better be on the safe side.

He takes a quick look over his shoulder.

                    HIRAM

                  (continuing)

You keep the pen.

He covertly and quickly takes it out and passes it to Joel.

                    JOEL

Hiram...!

Hiram goes off, in the direction of Moana.

MED. SHOT - BEHIND DRAPE

Moana comes through.

MOANA

He comes.

GEMMEL

Quick!

He leads the way down the corridor.

FULL SHOT - DANCE FLOOR

Hiram passes by Prentice and the others. He smiles pleasantly.

HIRAM

Hello, Mr. Prentice. Welcome to Hawaii.

PRENTICE

H-hello, Holliday.

Hiram keeps on going and lifts the drape and goes through.

MED. SHOT - BEHIND DRAPE

Hiram looks around and sees no one. He decides to proceed and–looking down–steps over the body on the floor.

INT. KITCHEN - MED. SHOT

Gemmel, Keoki and Moana are waiting tensely in a section of the kitchen. Gemmel gestures vigorously with his gun at a chef.

GEMMEL

Out.

The chef leaves hurriedly. Hiram enters through the swinging doors, and sees Moana.

                              HIRAM

Oh. There you are.

Gemmel steps forward.

                              GEMMEL

We meet again, Hiram Holliday.

                              HIRAM

Say! You were the man I saw at the hotel!

                              GEMMEL

We have not much time. The pen.

                              HIRAM

I know this is personal, but weren't you in jail?

                              GEMMEL

No jail can hold Gemmel. The pen.

                              HIRAM

I am unable to comply.

                              GEMMEL

Then you have crossed my path for the last time.

He raises his gun to fire as Hiram grabs a pot of beans from a stove
and throws it at him. Gemmel yells in pain and rage.

CLOSE SHOT - GEMMEL

He is clawing away the beans.

                              GEMMEL
                            (continuing)

Keoki! Cut him down!

FULL SHOT - KITCHEN

As Keoki comes after Hiram with his sword, Hiram grabs a potato masher from the wall...a large wooden one. He parries, then raps Keoki on the head and dashes through the swinging doors. Keoki comes after him.

INT. RESTAURANT - FULL SHOT - DANCE FLOOR

The MC is at the mike, still fighting to salvage the evening.

MC

In the peaceful islands, war is only a distant memory of a day gone by, remembered only today in the ceremony of the...

He breaks off and looks around. Hiram has burst through the drape behind him, wielding his potato masher.

MC

(continuing)

...of the...

Keoki bursts in, wielding his sword.

MC

(continuing)

...of the sword dance!

The MUSIC STRIKES UP. Keoki, realizing where he is, does a few ritual passes with the sword and is promptly rapped over the head by Hiram for his pains. With a cry, he takes after Hiram again.

TWO SHOT - PRENTICE AND DAVIES

They are staring at the strange dance.

DAVIES

You know that man?

PRENTICE

A bit eccentric but a nose for news.

FULL SHOT - DANCE FLOOR

Pursuing Hiram, Keoki leaps up on a large drum. As a concession to form, he does a few steps on the drum. Hiram raps him on his bare feet and with a howl, he jumps off in pursuit.

CLOSE SHOT - JOEL

He is staring open-mouthed.

FULL SHOT-DANCE FLOOR

Hiram now leaps up on the drum, jumping over the swings of Keoki.

CLOSE SHOT - AT DRAPE

Gemmel, still with a few stray beans, has lifted the drape and is taking a bead on Hiram.

FULL SHOT - DANCE FLOOR

Hiram sees Gemmel out of the corner of his eye and jumps off the drum. Keoki continues the attack.

MED. SHOT – JOEL

He has risen and is coming forward.

JOEL

(yelling)

He's trying to kill him! Hiram! Run! Run!!

FULL SHOT - DANCE FLOOR

Hiram gets in a few more raps with the masher, always in time with the MUSIC and dashes for the front exit. Keoki goes after him but bumps into Joel, who is by this time at the table of Prentice and Davies. The two large men fall heavily into the table, which flattens onto the floor.

MED. SHOT - AT TABLE

> PRENTICE

Smith!!

> DAVIES

You know him, too?

Joel tries to untangle himself from the roast pig.

> PRENTICE

Smith, you're fired!

> JOEL

Mr. Prentice, I quit!

He is by now on his feet with the pig in his arms, which he shoves at Prentice on his last speech. He stalks off.

TWO SHOT - PRENTICE AND DAVIES

Prentice, speechless, stares after Joel as Davies stares at him.

FADE OUT

SECOND COMMERCIAL

ACT TWO

FADE IN:

INT. HOTEL ROOM-DAY-FULL SHOT

Keoki is seated in a chair, while Moana paces impatiently. They are obviously waiting for someone. There is a SIGNAL RAP on the door. Keoki rises quickly, goes to the door and unlocks it, and lets in Gemmel. He seems strangely cheerful, in contrast with the tenseness of his confederates.

MOANA

You are a fool, Gemmel, to walk the streets in daylight.

GEMMEL

(tolerantly)

Ah?

KEOKI

After last night, the police are thick like ants.

GEMMEL

Ah.

He sits down and studies his nails.

MOANA

(impatiently)

Well? How do we get the pen? We never should have let go of it! We could freeze the harbor!

GEMMEL

You are a child. It is necessary for the American envoy himself to do it. Face it, my dear. The Americans will lose face in the Orient they will never regain. With their fleet frozen, our people can move as they will.

MOANA

Yes! Yes! But we have lost the pen!!

KEOKI

Let me go after Holliday.

GEMMEL

No. He is much too dangerous to be taken frontally. As you should know, Keoki.

MOANA

How, then?

GEMMEL

We will let the police do our work. I have dispatched to Mr. Holliday a rather secret document...a map of the Pearl Harbor mine fields.

KEOKI

What??

GEMMEL

I have also notified the police where to find Mr. Holliday and the document. After he is taken into custody, we simply search his room and pick up the pen. If he has it on him, the police will return it to its...ah...rightful owner...the American envoy.

MOANA

This will work, Gemmel?

GEMMEL

We have but to wait.

QUICK DISSOLVE:

INT. LANAI-DAY - FULL SHOT

CAMERA MOVES IN on Hiram and Joel, who are breakfasting in the Lanai and Surf Bar. At the moment, Joel is applying himself to the food, while Hiram is trying to figure out the pen.

HIRAM

I find this most curious, Joel.

JOEL

Mm?

HIRAM

Since a man was killed for it, some special significance must be attached. But what?

JOEL

Don't worry about the pen, Hiram. Worry about me. I not only missed my plane, I got fired.

HIRAM

Oh, I'm sure Mr. Prentice will have changed his mind by now. I find him stern but just.

WIDER ANGLE

Prentice steams into the picture.

PRENTICE

Holliday!

HIRAM

Oh, good morning, Mr. Prentice.

PRENTICE

Holliday, I want to know what you were doing last night!

Prentice grabs a chair and sits down, ignoring Joel.

HIRAM

Mr. Prentice, you remember Joel? Joel Smith?

Prentice does not turn.

PRENTICE

I'm trying to forget him. Holliday, what was that performance at the luau?

HIRAM

It was concerning this, Mr. Prentice.

He shows him the pen.

PRENTICE

Oh, you have it. Well, return it! The signing takes place at noon today!

HIRAM

It doesn't even write very well.

Hiram tries to write on the menu, but without success.

> HIRAM

Excuse me. I'll moisten the point.

He reaches over and dips the point in a fish bowl which is on the table.

CLOSE SHOT - FISH BOWL

There is a crack as the glass breaks and falls away, leaving the fish frozen in a block of ice.

MED. CLOSE SHOT - AT TABLE

Hiram looks at the bowl.

> HIRAM

Well, now.

> JOEL

> (touching it)

It's ice! Solid ice!

> PRENTICE

How did that happen??

> HIRAM

Gentleman, I believe we are in possession of a secret weapon.

> PRENTICE

We have to get it to the police, right now!

> HIRAM

A wise course.

He carefully puts the cap on the pen and puts it away in his pocket, rising.

HIRAM

(continuing)

I shall be with you as soon as I get my umbrella.

PRENTICE

This is no time for umbrellas, Holliday!

HIRAM

On the contrary, Mr. Prentice. I went out without it last night and almost paid with my life. Excuse me.

He goes off. Prentice and Joel look at each other, then turn their backs. A uniformed MESSENGER appears at the table.

MESSENGER

Mr. Holliday?

JOEL

I'll take it.

Prentice grabs the packet.

PRENTICE

I'll take it!

He puts it in his pocket as the messenger leaves. Joel is getting hotter.

JOEL

Look, Mr. Prentice...!

Prentice turns his back.

PRENTICE

I do not believe I know you.

As Joel fumes, two plainclothes OFFICERS come up to the table. One speaks to Prentice.

OFFICER

You're under arrest.

PRENTICE

What??

The other officer quickly reaches in Prentice's pocket and pulls out the package.

OFFICER

Come with us. Honolulu police.

He shows his badge as the second officer pulls Prentice up.

PRENTICE

But this is an outrage! I'm Harrison Prentice, publisher of the New York Chronicle! Smith! Tell these men who I am!

Joel is too mortal not to take his revenge.

JOEL

I never saw this man before in my life.

OFFICER

Come on!

The two carry off the wildly protesting Prentice, as Joel looks on with a diabolical smile.

INT. HIRAM'S HOTEL ROOM - FULL SHOT

Keoki and Moana are turning the room upside down in a search for the pen. They stop suddenly as they HEAR a key turn in the door.

Moana quickly signals Keoki to hide behind a drape. The door opens and Hiram enters.

MOANA

Come in, Hiram Holliday.

HIRAM

Thank you.

He enters, looking at the disorder of the room.

MOANA

I have been waiting for you.

HIRAM

Well, I'm glad you found something to do.

MOANA

The management sent me. It is time for your hula lesson. A new service for all guests.

HIRAM

That's most considerate. Just last night I had a free lesson in the sword dance.

MOANA

I had nothing to do with that! You believe me?

He hesitates. She continues.

MOANA

(continuing)

Yes?

HIRAM

I suppose the word I'm searching for is "no." Now, if I may get my umbrella.

He turns to pick it up. It is hung on a chair. Moana grabs him and whirls him around.

MOANA

Fool! You cannot hula with an umbrella!

CLOSE SHOT - DRAPE

Keoki's arm reaches out and takes the umbrella.

TWO SHOT - HIRAM AND MOANA

HIRAM

I have no intention of doing the hula. But if at some other time you would care to discuss the hamzah....

MOANA

Hamzah?

Hiram turns again for his umbrella and finds it gone.

HIRAM

Now, that's strange. I seem to have lost my umbrella.

MOANA

I feel you will find it, and soon.

As Hiram looks around, Keoki steps from behind the drape, behind Hiram, and fells him with a blow from the umbrella. Keoki quickly gets the pen from his pocket and holds it up with a smile.

                    MOANA

Why does Gemmel fear this man?

                                    DISSOLVE:

INT. HOTEL CORRIDOR - MED. SHOT

Joel stops at the door to Hiram's room. He knocks.

                    JOEL

Hiram?

He knocks again.

                    JOEL

                (continuing)

Hiram...are you in there?

After a moment, he tries the door and finds it open. He goes in.

REVERSE SHOT - AT DOOR

Joel reacts to what he sees in the room.

INT. HOTEL ROOM - CLOSE SHOT - HIRAM

He is sitting up, on the floor, with a dazed smile on his face.

                    JOEL (o.s.)

Hiram!

FULL SHOT - ROOM

Joel comes forward.

JOEL
(continuing)

What are you doing? I've been waiting over an hour and here you are, sitting on the floor!

HIRAM

Joel, I have met with a contretemps. Help me up.

TWO SHOT - HIRAM AND JOEL

Joel gets him on his feet.

JOEL

What happened?

HIRAM

(feeling his head)

I have paid the usual price of folly.

JOEL

You still have the pen?

Hiram feels in his coat pocket.

HIRAM

Unfortunately, no. What time is it?

Joel looks at his watch.

JOEL

Almost eleven.

HIRAM

The signing takes place at noon.

JOEL

You mean...? But we've got to stop it!...Get to the police!

HIRAM

Joel. If you were a policeman, would you believe that a fountain pen could freeze Pearl Harbor?

Joel realizes the situation.

JOEL

No. But what can we do?

HIRAM

I think we shall have to go to Hickam Field.

JOEL

Get out to the carrier in a plane? But the Air Force won't believe us either!

HIRAM

I didn't intend to tell them.

Joel recoils.

JOEL

Hiram! You're going to steal a plane??

HIRAM

Dire circumstances, Joel, call for dire measures. But I vastly prefer the term "borrow."

He picks up his umbrella and straightens the handle.

                              HIRAM
                            (continuing)

Shall we go?

QUICK DISSOLVE:

AERIAL VIEW - AIRCRAFT CARRIER – DAY - (STOCK)

DISSOLVE THRU:

EXT. DECK SECTION - FULL SHOT

An ADMIRAL is scanning the sky with binoculars, as Davies comes
rushing up.

                              DAVIES

Admiral! We're all ready for the signing! What's the delay!

The admiral lowers his glasses, although still looking at the sky.

                             ADMIRAL

We've had a radio report, Mr. Davies. A military plane has
been stolen from Hickam Field.

                              DAVIES

Well, what's that got to do with us?

                             ADMIRAL

Mr Davies. The plane is heading this way.

                              DAVIES

What??

                             ADMIRAL

The craft is armed. I have given orders to all guns to fire on
sight.

He returns his binoculars to his eyes, as Davies turns his face to the sky in alarm.

EXT. PLANE IN FLIGHT - LONG VIEW - (STOCK)

This is a Navy plane, if possible, going through some acrobatic manoeuvres.

INT. COCKPIT - CLOSE SHOT

This is a two-person plane, with Hiram at the controls and Joel directly behind him. Joel is bracing himself against the gyrations of the plane.

> JOEL
>
> Hiram! Level it out! I thought you knew how to fly this thing!

> HIRAM
>
> Oh, I do, Joel. That is, I know the aerodynamic principles.

> JOEL
>
> Just the principles?

> HIRAM
>
> Yes. From watching the flight of migrating robins. Oops!

Hiram grabs for the controls and Joel frantically braces himself as the plane goes into a roll. Hiram looks out the window of the tilting plane.

> HIRAM
>
> (continuing)
>
> Say. There's the carrier. I think I had better establish radio contact.

Hiram picks up the mic and turns a few knobs.

HIRAM

Hello, down there. Hello. This is Hiram Holliday up here. I'm sorry to bother you but I should like to land a stolen plane.

EXT. DECK SECTION - FULL SHOT

The admiral is still scanning the skies, having sighted Hiram. Davies is getting frantic.

DAVIES

Well, what are you waiting for?? Shoot him down!

The admiral snaps out an order.

ADMIRAL

Brewster!

An officer steps forward. The admiral continues.

ADMIRAL
(continuing)

Give all guns orders to–

A RADIOMAN comes running up.

RADIOMAN

Admiral!

The admiral turns.

RADIOMAN
(continuing)

Radio contact established, sir! Pilot identifies himself as Hiram Holliday...requests permission to land!

ADMIRAL

Holliday?

DAVIES

It's a reporter...the one who did the sword dance!

ADMIRAL

(to Davies)

Shall we shoot?

DAVIES

No! This is an election year!

The admiral turns to the radioman.

ADMIRAL

Grant permission to land.

INT. PLANE - CLOSE SHOT

Joel is still bracing himself.

JOEL

Hiram! You can't land this thing on that little deck!

He looks down.

EXT. CARRIER - AERIAL VIEW - (STOCK)

INT. PLANE - CLOSE SHOT

Hiram also looks down.

HIRAM

Joel, I believe you're right. But I fully intend to try.

JOEL

Hiram!

EXT. CARRIER DECK - FULL VIEW - (STOCK)

The landing officer is wig-wagging a plane in for a landing. At the last minute, he tries to wave it off but to no avail. The plane hits the deck, bounces and then noses over the side.

QUICK DISSOLVE:

EXT. DECK SECTION - FULL SHOT

The admiral and Davies are looking down, into the water.

DAVIES

Were they killed?

ADMIRAL

Unfortunately not.

(turning to his aide)

Brewster! I want those men brought here at once!

Brewster salutes and turns but then sees Hiram and Joel approaching, in the clutch of several sailors.

HIRAM

How do you do? I don't believe I quite made it.

He laughs at a pleasantry, dripping at the same time.

ADMIRAL

Holliday, I'm ordering you placed in irons, where you will no doubt spend the rest of your natural life. Have you anything to say?

HIRAM

Yes.

(to Davies)

I trust you still have the pen?

DAVIES

Why, yes.

HIRAM

Good.

He takes it from him.

HIRAM

(continuing)

You will not believe this except by demonstration. Excuse
me.

He takes off the admiral's cap, then turns to Joel.

HIRAM

(continuing)

Joel?

He holds out the cap to Joel who takes his coat and wrings it out,
filling the cap.

ADMIRAL

Stop!

HIRAM

One moment.

Hiram uncaps the pen and dips it in the water into the cap.

CLOSE SHOT - CAP

Joel turns it upside down and a block of ice falls out.

FULL SHOT - DECK

                           DAVIES

                          (staring)

Ice. Solid ice!

                            JOEL

It would have turned Pearl Harbor into a skating rink.

                          ADMIRAL

Incredible.

                           DAVIES

Mr. Holliday, on behalf of the United States Government
and the civilized world...thank you. What can we ever do to
repay you?

As he shakes Hiram's hand, Hiram looks down.

CLOSE SHOT - DECK

Hiram is standing in a small puddle.

CLOSE SHOT - HIRAM

                           HIRAM

Could I borrow a dry pair of trousers?

FADE OUT:

                     FINAL COMMERCIAL

FADE IN:

INT. LANAI - DAY-FULL SHOT

This is almost a duplication of the setting of the first scene. Joel is lounging with a tall drink, Hiram is studying his favorite author, Henry P. Codd, and the only difference is that Prentice is standing before them, consumed with exasperation and frustration.

PRENTICE

But why, why won't anybody tell me anything? Why?

JOEL

(sipping)

Military secret, Mr. Prentice.

PRENTICE

Military secret! That's all I hear! The Government practically orders me to take you back and to let you and Holliday do anything you want! They practically ordered me!

HIRAM

That was very nice of them.

PRENTICE

But what happened? All anybody will say is "secret weapon." What secret weapon? I don't want to be told everything...but just an inkling!

Hiram tries to change the subject. He refers to his book.

HIRAM

Joel...did I tell you Professor Codd's very interesting sidelight on the Hawaiian hamzah?

JOEL

No, what?

PRENTICE

Ah. The Hawaiian hamzah. No, don't tell me any more, Holliday. I don't want to know. The name is enough. The Hawaiian hamzah. Thank you.

HIRAM

Mr. Prentice...

Hiram looks at the smiling Prentice and decides not to spoil his bliss. Hiram and Joel exchange a shrug and a slight smile.

FADE OUT:

THE END

The Adventure of the Dancing Mouse

This was the seventh script commissioned but the eleventh episode broadcast. It first aired on NBC on 12 December 1956 and the BBC showed it on 11 August 1960, repeating it on 5 March the following year. It was written and produced by Philip Rapp and the episode itself was directed by George M Cahan. Cast included Ziva Rodann as Marlene, Ida Moore as Mrs Huckaby and Tor Johnson as Bandini.

FADE IN:

CLOSE SHOT - DAY - DOOR

This is the door to Prentice's office. It is lettered, "NEW YORK CHRONICLE, HARRISON PRENTICE, PUBLISHER."

DISSOLVE THRU:

FULL SHOT - PRENTICE'S OFFICE - DAY

CAMERA MOVES IN on PRENTICE, who is seated at his desk, barking into the phone in a high state of irritation.

PRENTICE

No, operator, no! I was talking to Mr. Joel Smith, in Genoa, Italy! You cut me off! Yes!

There is a slight pause, with Prentice drumming on his desk. The connection is then re-established.

PRENTICE

(continuing)

Smith? Prentice again...Yes, I got your last story. Smith, what's wrong with you? Am I spending thousands of dollars to have you make up things a child wouldn't believe? Hiram Holliday accused of blowing up the Rock of Gibraltar... engaged to a gypsy...fighting a duel with rapier and dagger... admit it...you made that up out of whole cloth!

CUT TO:

FULL SHOT - HOTEL ROOM

Joel and Hiram are in their hotel room in Genoa. Hiram is happily working on a camera of his own design, while Joel is suffering on the phone with Prentice.

JOEL

But it actually happened, Mr Prentice. I didn't make it up. He actually...

Joel holds the phone away from his ear as he is overwhelmed by Prentice.

CUT TO:

CLOSE SHOT - PRENTICE

PRENTICE

I wasn't born yesterday, Smith; or the day before. Blowing up the Rock of Gibraltar! That's not even good science fiction! What's wrong with you?

CUT TO:

CLOSE SHOT - JOEL

JOEL

(continuing)

I guess I lost my head, Mr. Prentice.

CUT TO:

CLOSE SHOT - PRENTICE

PRENTICE

(with satisfaction)

Yes, next time don't try to fool an old hand. Smith, don't send in another story without proof. Pictures, understand! And stay away from that Italian wine!

He hangs up.

CUT TO:

FULL SHOT - HOTEL ROOM

Joel slowly hangs up the phone.

> HIRAM

How's Mr. Prentice, Joel?

> JOEL

Hiram, if you blow up the Rock of Gibraltar, take a picture for me.

He holds up the contraption.

> JOEL

Your camera?

> HIRAM

Yes, I'm going out to a hunt with it.

> JOEL

What kind of hunt?

> HIRAM

A nature hunt. For the exclusive Italian pocket gopher, head-strong lemming, and the shy but determined field mouse. Care to come along?

> JOEL

I'll wait for you, Hiram. I don't feel up to any more excitement today.

HIRAM

Oh well, to quote from Julius Caesar, a river side.

He laughs up his little joke as he takes his camera and starts to go.

FADE OUT:

(FIRST COMMERCIAL)

FADE IN:

LONG VIEW - STREET CARNIVAL – DAY - STOCK

This show should establish a small carnival, with the characteristics of a Ferris Wheel and several circus tents.

MED. SHOT - HIRAM

Hiram is trying to get set for a shot with his camera to take a picture of a small animal on the ground. Which we do not see. Each time he almost gets the shot, the animal apparently moves, and Hiram has to stalk it for another try. Camera moves with Hiram as he goes.

WIDER ANGLE

In his pursuit, Hiram comes close to the wall of one of the carnival tents. The animal apparently goes underneath the tent wall and Hiram after looking around gets down and goes underneath the canvas.

REVERSE SHOT - INSIDE TENT

Hiram comes crawling under the canvas, sights his prey, and crawls cautiously toward it.

WIDER ANGLE

It can now be seen that two men are seated at a card table in the tent, with heads close together and talking inaudibly. They do not see Hiram as he is crawling in their direction behind a roll of canvas lying on the ground, nor can Hiram see them.

CLOSE SHOT - HIRAM

He gets ready to shoot, lying on the ground and pointing his camera up, as the subject is apparently on top of the roll of canvas.

MED. CLOSE SHOT - THE TWO MEN

One of them hears something and motions the other to silence. He slowly rises up to peer over the roll of canvas.

CLOSE SHOT – HIRAM - OTHERS' P.O.V.

Hiram snaps the picture and the flash bulb exploding as he does so.

HIRAM

Got it!

FULL SHOT - GROUP

The two men display extreme agitation. Thinking that Hiram has taken a picture of them, a picture they quite obviously do not want taken. The one directly facing Hiram's camera speaks; he is ALEX-ANDER, an imposing man with an aristocratic beard and wearing dark glasses.

ALEXANDER

He...he took a picture of both . . . of both of us!

The other man, of military bearing and a manner of command, takes in the situation quickly and makes a decision.

DRAGO

I think you had better go quickly.

He takes Alexander by the arm.

ALEXANDER

But you assured me, DRAGO! You...

DRAGO

Permit me.

He turns Alexander away from Hiram, and propels him toward the entrance of the tent.

DRAGO

Send back Bandini; but do not come back yourself. I will deal with him.

Alexander leaves hurriedly, and DRAGO turns to face Hiram.

DRAGO

(continuing)

So.

HIRAM

I must apologize for intruding. My name is Hiram Holliday and I...

DRAGO

I will take that picture.

He advances toward Hiram.

TWO SHOT - HIRAM AND DRAGO

HIRAM

I believe there has been a slight misunderstanding. You see, I didn't come in here to take a picture of you and your friend.

DRAGO

Ha.

HIRAM

Not that I don't consider you both photogenic. No indeed.

DRAGO

Give it to me.

HIRAM

I intruded because I was on the trail of one of the family Muridae.

DRAGO

Who?

HIRAM

He came under the tent and I followed him. In International Law, it is known as the doctrine of hot pursuit.

DRAGO

Pursuit of what???

HIRAM

A prime specimen of the Japanese dancing mouse.

DRAGO

Enough with the jokes!!

HIRAM

I am deadly serious. The Japanese dancing mouse actually only appears to dance because of a defect in his equilibrium...he is more to be pitied than jested at.

DRAGO looks at Hiram, and then decides to play for the time. He looks over his shoulder to see if aid is on the way and then he speaks to Hiram.

DRAGO

And what do you intend to do with your picture of the...ah... dancing mouse?

HIRAM

If it turns out well, I believe it should have considerable news value to my paper...the New York Chronicle.

DRAGO

So, you work for a newspaper.

HIRAM

Yes, naturally, I'll be glad to send you and the other gentleman several copies...if you'll give me your names and addresses.

DRAGO

Yes, I am sure would be happy to oblige.

HIRAM

Well, it was just a thought. Now if you'll excuse me...

DRAGO puts out an arm, stopping him.

DRAGO

The picture or you do not leave here alive!

He glances over his shoulder.

DRAGO
(continuing)

Bandini! Alla Prima! Subito!

FULL SHOT – BANDINI – THEIR P.O.V.

The carnival strong man, a monument of a man, is entering the tent.

TWO SHOT - HIRAM AND DRAGO

HIRAM

On second thought I believe I will give you the camera.

Hiram hands the surprised DRAGO the camera.

HIRAM

I can always make another one. Pardon me.

FULL SHOT - TENT

Hiram makes a fast exit the way he came in, as Bandini comes up quickly. DRAGO restrains him from going after Hiram.

DRAGO

Wait, his courage failed the camera.

He holds it up, then starts looking for the film inside.

DRAGO
(continuing)

The film? Where is the film?

Bandini takes it from his hands and crushes it in his powerful paws, then holds out the pieces for DRAGO.

BANDINI

There.

DRAGO

Tricked! There is no film, it develops its own pictures and he has the photograph!!! After him!!!

DISSOLVE:

ANOTHER TENT – DAY - FULL SHOT

One side of the small tent is rigged as a dressing table. As Alexander paces nervously, a girl in a costume of a harem dancer is putting on her make-up in front of the mirror. DRAGO enters the tent quickly and as the girl turns, we can see it is MARLENE.

ALEXANDER

(quickly)

You got the picture? You did get it??

DRAGO

He got away.

Marlene turns back to her mirror, exhibiting a profound indifference.

ALEXANDER

Got away?? How? How?

DRAGO

My men are after him and he cannot get off the grounds.

ALEXANDER

I warned you, DRAGO! I told you I should not come here. If the news is out that we are meeting together...

MARLENE

(without turning)

Then the chances of you returning as head of state to your former country aren't so bright.

ALEXANDER

Yes, but my need for a bungling chief of staff, General DRAGO shall be practically non-existent.

DRAGO

He came out of nowhere!

MARLENE

Who is he...this man who has made fools of you all?

DRAGO

An American...calling himself Hiram Holliday.

Marlene turns slowly.

MARLENE

Ah.

ALEXANDER

You know him? Is he dangerous, Marlene??

MARLENE

Better you had messed with the devil himself.

DRAGO

We have him bottled up. He cannot get to the police.

MARLENE

Hiram Holliday is not a man to go to the police.

DRAGO

(nodding)

A lone hand.

Marlene stands up.

MARLENE

A company of carabinieri would be far easier to deal with. You had best leave Hiram Holliday to Marlene.

ALEXANDER

You will find him?

MARLENE

No, he will find me.

She puts on her half-veil, in preparation for her number.

FULL SHOT - CARNIVAL GROUNDS

Hiram is seen walking furtively along the midway, looking back over his shoulder. He sees something a short distance away.

PHONE BOOTH - HIRAM'S P.O.V.

FULL SHOT - MIDWAY

Hiram heads for the phone booth and getting out a coin. He looks around to make sure he is not observed and is about to enter the booth when Mrs. Huckaby steps up. She is a rather elderly American tourist, from Iowa.

MRS. HUCKABY

I'm sorry, young man. This phone is in use.

Hiram looks in the booth.

CLOSE SHOT - BOOTH

It is obviously empty.

TWO SHOT - HIRAM AND MRS. HUCKABY

> HIRAM

It seems to be quite empty.

> MRS. HUCKABY

I'm expecting a call.

Having said this, she apparently considers the matter closed.

> HIRAM

Oh.

He looks off.

LONG SHOT - MIDWAY

Bandini is approaching and looking for Hiram.

MED. CLOSE SHOT - AT BOOTH

> HIRAM

I don't wish to appear discourteous, but....

> MRS. HUCKABY

The call is from my hotel. They're checking to see if I left my sun glasses on the washstand.

> HIRAM

Oh.

He looks off again.

LONG SHOT - MIDWAY

Bandini is closer, but he still has not spotted Hiram.

MED. CLOSE SHOT - AT BOOTH

Hiram is desperate and looks back at Mrs. Huckaby.

HIRAM

You wouldn't consider me making a call of short duration?

MRS. HUCKABY

My call is important.

HIRAM

Of course it is.

Against his principles, Hiram resorts to a subterfuge. He looks off.

HIRAM

(continuing)

Say, what is Nelson Eddy doing here?

MRS. HUCAKABY

(with great interest)

Nelson Eddy, where is he?

As she is peering off, Hiram quickly enters the booth and closes the door. He dials in a hurry.

MED. SHOT - AT BOOTH

Bandini comes in still looking. Mrs. Huckaby speaks to him.

MRS. HUCKABY

(continuing)

Do you see Nelson Eddy anywhere?

He stares at her and passes on.

MED. CLOSE SHOT - JOEL

Joel is in the hotel room reading. The phone rings and he picks it up.

JOEL

Hello, Hiram. How's the nature hunt?

CLOSE SHOT - HIRAM

HIRAM

I believe that I have a photograph that is of some value, Joel. At least there are a number of individuals who are trying to take it from me. Forcibly.

CLOSE SHOT - JOEL

He sits up suddenly and is alert.

JOEL

Where are you? The carnival grounds. All right then give me all the details. Shoot

INT. PHONE BOOTH - MED. CLOSE SHOT

HIRAM

Well, I…

He breaks off and Mrs. Huckaby is rapping on the door. Hiram turns back to the phone.

HIRAM

(continuing)

I'm sorry, Joel. Someone wants to use the phone.

CLOSE SHOT - JOEL

He reacts strongly.

JOEL

Someone wants to use the…Hiram, you can't hang up now.
I have to know, Hiram.

He jiggles the phone frantically, with no response and then holds
down the receiver for a second, then picks it up again.

JOEL

(continuing)

Operator, would you get me the police. Carabinieri! Carabinieri!!!

QUICK DISSOLVE:

CLOSE SHOT – POSTER - DAY

This is a bigger-than-life figure of Marlene in her harem dancer's
costume and painted on a canvas backdrop. CAMERA PULLS
BACK to reveal Hiram looking at the poster.

MRS. HUCKABY (o.s.)

Young man.

Hiram turns as the CAMERA ANGLE WIDENS to pick up Mrs
Huckaby.

HIRAM

Oh, I'm sorry about the phone. I....

Mrs Huckaby speaks in a tone of kindly reproach.

MRS. HUCKABY

With the glorious ark of antiquity all around you; do you
think you should be looking at that?

HIRAM

Oh, it's just that there is something very familiar about that young lady.

MRS. HUCKABY

Yes, there is. Wouldn't you rather view some old ruins?

HIRAM

Well, I'm very fond of old ruins but....

MARLENE (o.s.)

Hiram

Hiram looks in the direction of the voice.

EXT. PLATFORM - MED. CLOSE SHOT - HIRAM'S P.O.V.

Marlene has come out through the canvas onto the platform. Her veil half-covers her face. She speaks again beckoning at the same time.

MARLENE

Hiram.

MED. SHOT - GROUND LEVEL

Bandini comes up behind Hiram silently and has taken him by the seat of the trousers.

BANDINI

The young lady is waiting, don't keep her.

Marlene goes through the opening back into the tent. Bandini starts to propel Hiram forward, reaches into his coat and pulls out the photograph. Which he hands to Mrs. Huckaby.

DRAGO

(to Bandini)

Search him!

HIRAM

If compelled could resist.

He has his umbrella at the ready.

DRAGO

Bandini!

MARLENE

No, not here!

DRAGO

Where then?

MARLENE

A place less public and more quiet. There my dear Hiram; I
shall be more persuasive. The Tunnel of Love.

HIRAM

With you alone?

DRAGO

Hardly, Bandini and I will act as chaperones.

HIRAM

(brightening)

Thank you, that's quite a relief.

Bandini and DRAGO look at one another, as we–

DISSOLVE:

EXT. CARNIVAL GROUNDS – DAY - FULL SHOT

Joel and a uniformed policeman are standing at the end of the Tunnel of Love. As the CAMERA MOVES IN, it can be seen that the policeman has lost interest in his mission and while Joel is still looking around for Hiram.

> POLICEMAN

Signor, your friend had perhaps gone home, eh?

> JOEL

He wouldn't do that. Because, on the phone he told me he was in trouble. Something about a picture.

> POLICEMAN

Ah, he was on the trail of those who stole the Mona Lisa, yes?

> JOEL

All right, I know we've looked all over but can't we just wait a little longer? Hiram Holliday isn't the type to...

Mrs. Huckaby comes on addressing the policeman.

> MRS. HUCKABY

Oh, are you a policeman?

> POLICEMAN

Si, signora.

MRS. HUCKABY

Well, I want to report a missing pair of sunglasses.

JOEL

Now, just a minute.

MRS. HUCKABY

(ignores Joel completely)

I may have left them back at my hotel on the washstand; but when I was phoning there this rather flighty young man came along and I never found out if...

POLICEMAN

Signora, I should suggest that you...

Joel is getting hot under the collar.

JOEL

(to policeman)

A man's life may be in danger here and you're talking about sunglasses!

POLICEMAN

Signora, I....

MRS. HUCKABY

I may have left them in Monte Carlo but I don't think so.

POLICEMAN

Signora...

JOEL

(to policeman)

Would you like me to take this whole thing to the American consulate?

Mrs. Huckaby sees him for the first time.

MRS. HUCKABY

Now, why didn't I think of that?

POLICEMAN

(almost shouting)

Signora! Signora!

At his moment they hear the sound of a boat bumping along through the tunnel. It was coming toward the exit. They turn in a different direction.

TUNNEL EXIT - THEIR P.O.V.

A long boat comes into view. The water in which it floats is not visible; due to the boards on either side. In the front seat of the boat a young Italian couple are locked in a tight embrace. Then there were a couple of vacant seats come into view and Hiram and Marlene. Marlene has her back turned and Hiram has a disheveled look. In the seat directly behind are Bandini and DRAGO. Hiram sees Joel.

HIRAM

Hello, Joel.

CLOSE SHOT - JOEL

He reacts in amazement.

JOEL

Hiram!!!

MED. SHOT - BOAT

MARLENE

(to Hiram)

Darling, you were wonderful. We must go around again!

She enfolds him in a close embrace as the boat is carried out of sight. (Marlene has changed to a low-cut blouse and skirt.)

MED. SHOT - GROUP

The policeman turns to Joel.

POLICEMAN

Is that your friend?

JOEL

Yes, but...

POLICEMAN

This is the trouble he is in?

JOEL

Well, he...

POLICEMAN

In Italy, every man wishes for such trouble. You will come with me to the station please?

As Joel allows himself to be guided off by the policeman, CAMERA STAYS with Mrs. Huckaby, who is looking sadly in the direction of the departed Hiram.

MRS. HUCKABY

I wonder why he gave me that postcard?

FADE OUT

END OF ACT ONE

ACT TWO

FADE IN:

CARNIVAL GROUNDS – DAY - FULL SHOT

This is a view of the midway. In the vicinity of the telephone booth. CAMERA CLOSES IN on the booth, revealing Hiram talking into the phone and at the same time looking around for possible pursuers.

HIRAM

Joel, this is Hiram. I thought that I could reach you at the police station.

SCREEN SPLITS to show Joel at a desk in the police station. The policeman from the first act is nearby.

JOEL

Hiram, where are you?

HIRAM

(looking around)

I have temporarily excluded my pursuers.

JOEL

The girl too?

HIRAM

I have not time to defend my reputation, Joel. Listen carefully, I think I know the identity of the man in those pictures I took while photographing a Japanese dancing mouse.

JOEL

What??

HIRAM

Never mind, his name is Alexander and he is a former dictator of Bulgaria.

JOEL

Hiram, that man is in Paris. He's not allowed out of France.

HIRAM

Nevertheless, I took a picture of him in Genoa. It seems that an international coup is in the making.

JOEL

(a little doubtful)

Have you got the picture?

HIRAM

I have it in a safe place.

JOEL

Well, if you can prove it, Hiram...

HIRAM

Just call the Paris police, Joel. Then call me back here. The number is...

(looks at the phone)

one, two, five, seven, nine, Goodbye.

He hangs up.

FULL SHOT - POLICE STATION

An Italian police lieutenant is in the room along with the policeman from the carnival and they both look at Joel. He starts to explain without much conviction.

JOEL

That was Hiram Holliday.

LIEUTENANT

Si?

JOEL

It seems that while photographing a Japanese dancing mouse, he also took a picture of Alexander of Bulgaria plotting a revolution.

POLICEMAN

(nodding)

Very likely.

JOEL

We are to call the Paris police. Just to make sure it was Alexander.

LIEUTENANT

Alexander the man or Alexander the dancing mouse?

JOEL

The man and then call him back, Hiram.

POLICEMAN

Hiram the man.

JOEL

Yes.

A long look passes between the policeman and the lieutenant. They then look at Joel who shrugs defensively. The lieutenant reluctantly picks up the phone.

LIEUTENANT

Prefecture de police, Paris.

FULL SHOT - CARNIVAL GROUNDS-AT THE PHONE BOOTH

Hiram is waiting nervously beside the phone booth as Mrs. Huckaby comes into the picture and starts for the booth.

MRS. HUCKABY

How do you do?

HIRAM

Excuse me, but where are you going to use the phone?

MRS. HUCKABY

Yes, I am.

HIRAM

I hate to be a nuisance, but I have got a very important call coming in.

> MRS. HUCKABY

Another social engagement?

> HIRAM

No, it's about a man who is trying to overthrow the government. I took his picture while photographing a dancing mouse.

> (a long pause)

I suppose you find that hard to believe.

> MRS. HUCKABY

> (straight)

No, it sounds very logical.

Hiram looks at her and the PHONE RINGS. Hiram jumps for it and as he enters the booth, Bandini comes on the scene, and tries to open the door of the booth. Hiram is holding it against him and trying to answer at the same time.

> HIRAM

Hello, Hello.

FULL SHOT - POLICE STATION

Joel is on the phone with the lieutenant and the policeman is standing over him.

> JOEL

Hello, Hiram are you there? What's wrong Hiram?

MED. CLOSE SHOT - BOOTH

Hiram is still trying to hold out Bandini.

HIRAM

Just a minute Joel.

He drops the receiver and blocks the door of the phone booth by bracing his umbrella against the other wall of the booth. (The door is the type that is hinged in the middle and opens in.) Hiram now picks up the phone again.

HIRAM

Go ahead, Joel. Did they call Paris?

MED. SHOT - GROUP AT THE STATION

JOEL

Yes, they called Paris. Hiram, the French police says Alexander never left the country. Hiram are you still there?

MED. SHOT - BOOTH

Bandini was unable to get into the booth and is now in the act of picking up the booth. Hiram in the booth. He is rocking the booth off its foundations. Hiram sees what is happening then speaks into the phone.

HIRAM

I'm still here, Joel but I have the feeling I am about to be cut off. I think you had better come out here.

MED. SHOT - AT THE STATION

JOEL

Hiram! Hiram!!

He jiggles the phone on the hook.

MED. SHOT - BOOTH

Bandini now has the booth up on his back and is walking off with it. Hiram inside speaks into the phone.

HIRAM

Joel?

The phone is dead. With a slight shrug, Hiram hangs up.

FULL SHOT - CARNIVAL GROUNDS

Hiram and the booth are carried right by Mrs. Huckaby. Hiram sees her.

CLOSE SHOT - HIRAM

He waves at her.

CLOSE SHOT - MRS. HUCKABY

She waves back at him and looks at him doubtfully.

MRS. HUCKABY

What an odd way to travel.

FULL SHOT - MIDWAY

Hiram and the booth are being carried along on the back of Bandini and at the same time people turn and stare.

INT. BOOTH - CLOSE SHOT

Hiram looks around for some way out. He then takes his umbrella, removes it as a brace, and jabs the point through the glass. Against the lower back of Bandini.

MED. SHOT - MIDWAY

Bandini suddenly drops the booth with a howl. The booth falls on its side and the door opens. Hiram scrambles out. Bandini whirls and tries to get to him, but falls over the booth. Hiram gives him a sharp rap on the head with his umbrella as he goes down. Hiram than starts to stroll off casually, looks back and sees Bandini getting up.

FULL SHOT - MIDWAY

Hiram than takes off in a run, turning the corner and disappearing from view.

QUICK DISSOLVE:

MIDWAY-DAY - FULL SHOT

It is a few minutes later. CAMERA PICK UP Bandini and DRAGO are searching for Hiram. DRAGO puts his hand on Bandini's arm pointing off. They started going forward.

MED. SHOT-HIRAM - THEIR P.O.V.

He has seen them at the same time that they have seen him. He turns to find himself next to a shooting gallery. Several men are lined up at the counter with rifles; shooting at the moving targets. Hiram steps up to the counter, takes out a coin, gives it to the attendant and receives a rifle in return. He turns to face Bandini and DRAGO after putting his umbrella on the counter.

TWO SHOT - BANDINI AND DRAGO

They stop as they see Hiram with a rifle.

MED. SHOT - SHOOTING GALLERY

The attendant taps Hiram on the shoulder and points to the targets. Indicating that he should aim in that direction. Hiram nods his apologies and shoots. There is the CLANG of a bull's-eye.

TWO SHOT - BANDINI AND DRAGO

They started forward again.

AT GALLERY

Hiram turns to face his antagonists and the attendant takes hold of the end of his gun swinging it around to the target again. Hiram does not turn with it, the gun is now pointing over his shoulder. He fires without looking and there is the CLANG of a bull's-eye. The attendant then stares at him as do the other marksmen. Hiram smiles to indicate that it was nothing. He fires again and there is another CLANG with the same reaction. Beginning to enjoy it, Hiram fires twice more with two more CLANGS. All are now staring at him in open admiration. He pulls the trigger again but the only result is a CLICK. He CLICKS several times more before realizing he is out of bullets.

TWO SHOT - BANINI AND DRAGO

They smile and close in.

FULL SHOT - AT THE GALLERY

As the two men close in on Hiram he looks around for an avenue of escape. Just as they are about to reach him he quickly vaults over the counter.

MED. SHOT - INSIDE GALLERY

The attendant has gotten down a huge doll which he is offering to Hiram as a prize. Just as Hiram vaults the counter.

HIRAM

Thank you.

He takes the doll, grabs his umbrella from the counter and vanishes through the back entrance to the gallery. DRAGO and Bandini are trying to climb over the counter after him.

QUICK DISSOLVE:

EXT. TENT-DAY - MED. CLOSE SHOT

Hiram comes quickly into the picture and looks around. Feeling the hot breath of pursuit close behind. He looks at the tent wall then makes a decision and dives under the tent. (He still carries the doll.)

INT. TENT - REVERSE SHOT

Hiram is crawling underneath.

> MARLENE
>
> (o.s.)

Hiram

Hiram looks, then scrambles to his feet as CAMERA PULLS BACK to reveal Marlene. This is her dressing room and she rises from her seat in front of the mirror. She has changed back to her harem girl costume.

> HIRAM

Pardon the intrusion.

> MARLENE

You could not stay away from me.

She comes close to him.

> HIRAM

No, but I tried.

> MARLENE

What drove you to my arms?

> HIRAM

Your friend. He's bigger than both of us.

He looks around apprehensively. Marlene indicates the doll.

MARLENE

For me, Hiram?

Hiram looks down having forgotten what he was carrying.

HIRAM

Oh, just a little something I picked up along the way.

He gives it to her.

MARLENE

You are sweet and I shall help you.

HIRAM

If it's all the same to you I'd rather you wouldn't bother.

Marlene comes even closer, putting her hands on Hiram's shoulders.

MARLENE

I am not all bad, Hiram. I need only the aid of a good man.

HIRAM

I shall be glad to recommend a capable psychiatrist.

Marlene suddenly stares off. She lowers her voice to an urgent whisper.

MARLENE

They are coming. Go through there quickly.

She turns him around, leading him to a tent flap.

HIRAM

(politely)

Is that the snake concession?

MARLENE

It is the dressing room of another performer. He will not show up tonight. He is drinking. Put on his costume.

HIRAM

A suitable disguise, I trust.

MARLENE

They will never know you and you will be safe, dear Hiram. Safe.

HIRAM

Not believing it for a second, I will go.

He goes through the tent flap. Marlene listens at the flap for a moment and then goes quickly to the exit and out.

QUICK DISSOLVE:

EXT. MIDWAY – DAY - FULL SHOT

CAMERA PICKS UP DRAGO and Bandini near the shooting gallery. They are looking around for Hiram as they are joined by Marlene. She wears the costume of the previous scene.

MARLENE

Have you found him, Drago?

DRAGO

Not yet. He slips through our fingers and is like a quicksilver.

MARLENE

You need not worry.

DRAGO

Why?

MARLENE

Hiram Holliday will leave his clothes, which we can search to our leisure and leap to his death from a hundred foot tower.

DRAGO

What madness is this??

MARLENE

I told you leave Hiram Holliday to me and watch.

She points off. DRAGO and Bandini gaze in the direction indicated.

FULL SHOT - ANOTHER PART OF MIDWAY

All of the midway crowd has gathered around the base of a tall tower beside a very small tank of water. The ANNOUNCER steps to the cleared space in the middle of the crowd.

ANNOUNCER

Signore e signoras! In all of Europe, in all of the world the most great act of daring! A dive from one hundred and twenty feet.

(points up)

Into the tank only three feet deep!! The great Guido!!!

He motions and all eyes turn.

EXT. TENT - MED. CLOSE SHOT

The flap opens. Hiram steps out wearing a robe over a swimsuit and a man's bathing cap on his head. He looks somewhat bewildered at the applause.

MED. SHOT - GROUP AT THE SHOOTING GALLERY

Marlene, still looking off toward Hiram and speaks to DRAGO.

MARLENE

What did I tell you?

BANDINI

But will he go up?

DRAGO

I will see that he does.

He goes to the counter and takes a rifle, getting ready to point it at Hiram.

FULL SHOT - TOWER AREA

The announcer goes over to Hiram and leads him to the base of the tower.

TWO SHOT - ANNOUNCER AND HIRAM

ANNOUNCER

You are the substitute for Guido?

Hiram looks up very doubtful.

HIRAM

I suppose I am.

He walks over and peers at the small tank.

ANNOUNCER

You know your business? The dive is not easy.

HIRAM

Well, I've never tried it before but...

He looks off.

SHOOTING GALLERY - HIRAM'S POV

DRACO is aiming the rifle at Hiram.

TWO SHOT - ANNOUNCER AND HIRAM

ANNOUNCER

But what??

HIRAM

But, I suppose the only way to learn is to do it.

The announcer helps him off with his robe and Hiram starts up the ladder.

MED. SHOT - OUTER EDGE OF CROWD

Mrs. Huckaby is standing, looking up, as Joel approaches her with the lieutenant and policeman in tow.

JOEL

Excuse me.

Mrs. Huckaby turns to him.

JOEL

(continuing)

We are looking for my friend, the one who came out of the tunnel of love?

MRS. HUCKABY

Oh, yes. He's a friend of yours?

JOEL

Yes, have you seen him?

MRS. HUCKABY

Of course.

She turns to the policeman.

MRS. HUCKABY

(continuing)

Have you found my sunglasses yet, officer?

JOEL

Please, I have the feeling my friend is in danger and I.....

MRS. HUCKABY

Danger? Hardly. He's just out for a good time.

LIEUTENANT

You have seen him?

MRS. HUCKABY

Of course, there he is.

She points up. They follow her gaze.

MED. SHOT – TOWER - THEIR POV

Hiram is climbing about twenty feet up.

CLOSE SHOT - JOEL

He reacts sharply.

MED. CLOSE SHOT - GROUP

Joel turns to the police.

                          JOEL

You've got to stop him! He'll kill himself!

The lieutenant shrugs.

                       LIEUTENANT

If he does not jump nothing is lost. If he jumps he is insane.
Nothing is lost.

He watches calmly as Joel slowly turns his horrified gaze back to the
tower.

CLOSE SHOT - HIRAM

He stops climbing and looks down.

CROWD - HIRAM'S POV

CLOSE SHOT - HIRAM

He looks off toward DRAGO.

DRAGO - HIRAM'S POV

He is pointing the rifle.

CLOSE SHOT - HIRAM

He starts up again.

TWO SHOT - JOEL AND MRS. HUCKABY

Mrs. Huckaby speaks with reluctant admiration.

                     MRS. HUCKABY

I don't entirely approve of your friend, but he certainly does
have fun.

Joel turns and looks at her.

FULL SHOT - TOWER

Hiram has just about reached the top. He attains it and climbs out on the platform.

CLOSE SHOT - HIRAM

He looks down.

CROWD - HIRAM'S POV

It is a long way down.

CLOSE SHOT - HIRAM

Having a touch of vertigo, he starts for the ladder to climb down again.

CLOSE SHOT - DRAGO

He fires.

CLOSE SHOT - HIRAM

He jumps back from the ladder as there is the SOUND of a ricochet. After recovering himself, he looks down again.

TANK AND CROWD - HIRAM'S POV

CLOSE SHOT - HIRAM

He thinks it over.

HIRAM

Well, now.

CLOSE SHOT - ANNOUNCER

He gestures upward.

ANNOUNCER

The Great...Guido!!!

There is the SOUND of a drum roll, which continues over CUTS of Joel, Mrs. Huckaby, the police, DRAGO, and Marlene are all staring up.

FULL SHOT - TOWER

A splash goes up from Hiram's dive into the tank. Joel and the police rush forward and followed more leisurely by Mrs. Huckaby.

CLOSE SHOT - EDGE OF TANK

Hiram's face appears over the edge and dripping of water. CAMERA PULLS BACK as Joel rushes up.

HIRAM

Hello, Joel.

JOEL

Hiram, are you all right?

HIRAM

Say, that was fun.

JOEL

(horrified)

Fun??

HIRAM

I may try it again.

He climbs out of the tank and down onto the ground.

JOEL

Never mind trying it again where's the picture? The picture of the dictator?

HIRAM

I believe it's perfectly safe.

CLOSE SHOT - HIRAM

Being a philosopher, he shrugs, as we:

FADE OUT.

COMMERCIAL

FADE IN:

INT. HOTEL ROOM – DAY - FULL SHOT

As in the first scene Joel is suffering on the phone with Prentice; as Hiram is happily checking over a new camera of his own design.

JOEL

I know the story sounds fantastic Mr. Prentice but there is proof. Just contact this small boy in Des Moines; his name is Orville Huckaby. He has the picture in the foreground, is a Japanese dancing mouse and Hello, Hello, Mr. Prentice?

Joel sadly replaces the receiver and turns to Hiram.

JOEL
(continuing)

He hung up on me.

HIRAM

I'm sorry, Joel. But the plot was foiled and that's the important thing, isn't it?

JOEL

Oh, sure. Going somewhere, Hiram?

Hiram is standing, ready to go.

> HIRAM

Trying out my new camera. On a nature hunt with Mrs. Huckaby.

> JOEL

Oh.

> HIRAM

Care to come along?

> JOEL

I don't think so.

As Hiram starts off, Joel turns INTO THE CAMERA.

> JOEL

> (continuing)

I suppose I should, but somehow I just don't have the strength.

FADE OUT

-THE END-

The Adventure of the Moroccan Hawk-Moth

This was the fourteenth script to be commissioned and the fifteenth episode to air. It was broadcast by NBC on 9 January 1957 and on the BBC on 22 August 1960, with a repeat on 20 July 1961. It was written by Siegfried Herzig and Joel Malcolm Rapp, with the resulting episode directed by the latter's father, Philip Rapp.

FADE IN:

STOCK SHOT MONTAGE – MOROCCO - DAY

A muezzin in a minaret calling the faithful to prayer, after which we hear a thread of high-pitched MUSIC played on a flute, followed by shots depicting a picturesque city, ringed by desert and guarded by a fort. A tableau of mosques, minarets, and domed palaces gives us the feeling of intrigue and adventure.

DISSOLVE:

EXT. HOTEL - DAY (STOCK)

A continental hotel in Morocco. If possible, this should be a SHOT which culminates with a PAN toward the top of the hotel.

DISSOLVE THROUGH:

FULL SHOT - EXT. HOTEL ROOF

HIRAM is busy with a complicated contraption as JOEL, dressed in tropical clothes, enters the scene.

TWO SHOT – HIRAM AND JOEL

JOEL

What's that thing, Hiram?

HIRAM

Hello, Joel. I have high hopes of capturing Telea Sphingdae.

JOEL

Who?

HIRAM

Telea Sphingdae, or the spotted Moroccan hawk-moth. Often mistaken for the monarch butterfly, although never by the female moth.

He laughs slightly.

JOEL

How does your moth-trap work?

HIRAM
(eyes shining)

I put a leaf of cabbage, Telea's favorite staple, on the postage scale. When the moth alights on the delicate balance, his slight weight pulls the string, which releases the net, and the capture is complete.

He is going through the above actions as he is talking, peeling a leaf off a head of cabbage and putting it on the balance.

JOEL

What's the clock for?

HIRAM

An alarm, activated by the falling net. To let me know when Telea has swooped down from the skies.

JOEL

Hiram. Come over here.

He leads Hiram away from the trap, to the edge of the roof.

HIRAM

Yes, Joel?

> JOEL

Look out there. Morocco, the land of intrigue and adventure. What are you doing?...Trapping butterflies.

> HIRAM

Moths, Joel. I feel certain that our paper would be vitally interested in a series on the metamorphic cycle of Telea Sphingdae .

Joel looks at him.

> JOEL

Do you?

> HIRAM

Why not?

Both turn at the SOUND OF THE ALARM.

FULL SHOT-ROOF

Hiram and Joel come back to the trap.

> HIRAM

Joel!

CLOSE SHOT - TRAP

The net now encloses a hunting falcon.

MED. CLOSE SHOT - AT TRAP

> JOEL

> (staring)

What's that thing?

HIRAM

It appears that I have outdone myself. Instead of a hawk-moth, I have netted a hawk. More exactly, a hunting falcon.

JOEL

Where did he come from?

HIRAM

I have no idea. But where the ordinary falcon is exclusively carnivorous, this bird is obviously a vegetarian. Would you hold this, Joel?

He hands Joel the cabbage he has been holding, and takes a handkerchief from his pocket, wrapping it around his wrist.

JOEL

What's that for?

HIRAM

A makeshift for the traditional falconer's glove.

He raises the net and lifts out the bird on his wrist.

JOEL

You're sure you know how to handle that thing?

HIRAM

Of course, Joel. I've read Professor Gosling from cover to cover. Say, this is interesting.

Hiram takes from the bird's beak a large, ornate signet ring.

INSERT - RING

BACK TO SCENE

Joel and Hiram are looking at the ring.

JOEL

That bird's no vegetarian...he's a kleptomaniac.

HIRAM

If I'm not mistaken, this ring bears the seal of the 14th Caid of Mekra-bel-Ksiri.

JOEL

Oh, sure.

Hiram is studying the ring intensely. He presses it, and the heavy rounded top of the ring flips open, revealing a chamber inside. Hiram takes a piece of paper from the chamber.

HIRAM

Well. This is interesting.

(reading)

"Welcome. The palace, Joel. Of Yussuf Ben Mahid...the 14th Caid."

JOEL

I saw the Palace. It's a new jewelry store opening down the street.

HIRAM

Really?

JOEL

Really. Advertising. How about hunting up a restaurant? I'm starved.

He looks at the cabbage speculatively, takes a piece and chews it.

HIRAM

I'll join you later, Joel. I want to bait up again.

Joel tosses him the cabbage.

JOEL

Strictly moth-food. I'll see you later.

He goes off, as Hiram busies himself with the trap, with the hawk still on his wrist.

AHMED'S VOICE

Pardon, sidi.

ANOTHER ANGLE

Hiram turns, to see the owner of the voice. He is AHMED, emissary from the Caid, clothed in the garments of the Berber. He moves to Hiram's side.

HIRAM

How do you do?

AHMED

You got the message? I come from the palace.

HIRAM

I wish the best of luck on your new enterprise.

AHMED

With you, O Hawk of the Desert, we will have no need of luck. The Caid awaits.

HIRAM

For me?

AHMED

For you. Come.

He starts off.

CLOSE SHOT-HIRAM

He looks after Ahmed, then to his trap, gives his characteristic shrug and starts after his guide.

FADE OUT

FIRST COMMERCIAL

FADE IN:

EXT. PALACE-DAY (STOCK)-AVAILABLE SHOTS

A rich looking palace.

DISSOLVE

KING INT. CAID'S RECEPTION ROOM-DAY-FULL SHOT

A luxurious, richly appointed room. The walls are hung with Kumia swords and ancient tapestries, and a servant girl and a bare-torsoed guard move about the room from time to time. The CAID is seated cross-legged on the floor. Next to him, feeding large purple grapes into his mouth, is the head of the harem, YASMIN, a gorgeous girl dressed in the scanty costume. The Caid himself, although definitely a Berber, has a European polish.

CLOSER SHOT - CAID AND YASMIN

As she pops another grape into his face.

YASMIN

You are content, my Caid?

CAID

Quite, my dear Yasmin.

He reacts disgustedly to a KNOCK on the door.

CAID

Enter.

MED. SHOT

To include the door. It opens, and Ahmed enters. He moves across the room to the Caid and bows deeply.

MED. SHOT - AHMED, THE CAID, YASMIN

CAID

He is here?

Ahmed nods, and hands the ring to the Caid.

CAID

(smiling)

Good. Bring him in.

AHMED

Caid, there is something unusual...

CAID

(angrily)

Careful how you speak, son of a camel! The Desert Hawk is the most powerful man in all the East. It is the most fortunate for us he is our ally in this matter.

AHMED

But his appearance. It is not what you would expect.

CAID

Fool! He is forced to change his appearance constantly. For every grain of sand on the desert there is a pair of eyes which seek the Hawk and a pair of hands which itch for the price of his head. Bring him in!

AHMED

Yes, sire.

He bows again and backs out of the SCENE.

CAID

Yasmin. Back to the harem.

YASMIN

But, sire, I have long yearned to see the Desert Hawk...

CAID

Yes. I know. Go!

She rises and moves out toward a door to the right, and exits.

ANOTHER ANGLE

As the other door opens, and Ahmed re-enters, leading Hiram, who is carrying the Hawk on one hand and his umbrella in the other. The hawk is hooded with a handkerchief.

AHMED

Caid Yusuff Ben Mahid - The Desert Hawk.

CLOSER ANGLE

As Ahmed backs out, and Hiram, smiling happily, moves toward the Caid who is bowing.

> HIRAM
>
> (in Arabic)

How do you do?

> CAID
>
> (in Arabic)

It is my pleasure, O Hawk.

> (in English)

Welcome to my humble palace.

> HIRAM

Be it ever so humble, there's no place like a palace.

He laughs it up, as the Caid looks closely at Hiram. He reacts, as he understands Ahmed's confusion. He continues to stare.

> HIRAM

Is there something wrong?

> CAID
>
> (suddenly understanding)

Of course. The fierce Hawk assumes the guise of the timid sparrow to confuse his enemies.

Hiram smiles, and strokes the falcon.

> HIRAM

I thought he was a rather robust specimen myself. Besides, I doubt if he has any enemies. He's a vegetarian.

CAID

The Hawk's wit is as sharp as the talons of his namesake. But there is not time for idle jesting.

HIRAM

Oh?

CAID

We strike tonight!

HIRAM

We do?

CAID

Everything is in readiness and now that the Hawk of the Desert is here...

HIRAM

I'm afraid I must apologize.

CAID

For what?

HIRAM

My face. You see, my features are such that people constantly think they have met me previously.

CAID

But I have never seen you before.

HIRAM

Oh?

CAID

But you carry your identification. The hawk, trained to bear my ring to his master.

HIRAM

I can explain that. He stopped off for a bite of cabbage.

CAID

Cabbage?

HIRAM

I trapped him. While trying to catch a moth.

CAID

You carry your disguise quite far. Even to adopting the American humor.

HIRAM

Thank you.

The Caid walks around Hiram, surveying him.

CAID

A perfect disguise. The umbrella, the hat, the glasses...the perfect model of a fatuous American. I compliment you.

HIRAM

A great deal of the credit must go to my parents.

CAID

It is good that your reputation for the eccentric has preceded you. Did I think for one moment you were not the Desert Hawk...

His eyes tell the story, and then he laughs jovially. Hiram joins in politely.

CAID

(resuming)

To business. My ring.

HIRAM

Of course.

He takes it out of his pocket and gives it to the Caid, who flips it open.

CAID

Into here will go a powerful explosive...no larger than a pea. Your Western technology.

He smiles, and Hiram smiles back.

CAID

(continuing)

It can be smuggled into the fort with no difficulty.

HIRAM

Any particular fort?

CAID

(smiling)

Ha. The one where they are meeting.

HIRAM

(not understanding, but agreeable)

Oh.

CAID

They have kept their secret of their meeting well, but not well enough. The four most powerful men in the Western world, O Hawk.

HIRAM

Really?

CAID

Wiped out at one blow by the most powerful man in the East.

HIRAM

Sounds like quite a fellow. Who is he?

CAID

You.

HIRAM

Well now.

CAID

Until the time, there is everything here for your comfort.

HIRAM

I would like to get a message to a friend of mine.

CAID

It is done.

He claps his hands. Yasmin appears almost immediately, and bows.

CAID

You will do the bidding of the Hawk.

                    YASMIN

                    (staring)

That is the Hawk?

                    CAID

A master of disguise, eh? A master!

He laughs hugely, to which Hiram joins to a lesser degree.

DISSOLVE:

MED. SHOT - EXT. STREET-DAY

Joel is stopped by the cart of a street vendor, negotiating for some food, and has some difficulty getting through.

                    JOEL

Look. How about some roast lamb? Mechoni?

The vendor dips a spoon into a pot.

                    VENDOR

Couscous?

                    JOEL

No. No, I don't want any couscous. How about Mutton stew... tajine ohmar?

The vendor dips into another pot.

                    VENDOR

Couscous?

                    JOEL

No. No couscous. Chicken and honey? Djedjad imer?

The vendor goes into another pot.

VENDOR

Couscous?

JOEL

No! How about roast stuffed kid? Knaroof mahsky?

The vendor does his routine.

VENDOR

Couscous?

Yasmin, wearing a veil, appears behind Joel, tapping him on the shoulder. He does not turn.

JOEL

(over his shoulder)

Just a minute.

(to vendor)

Egg kebab? Aijet beythat?

VENDOR

Couscous?

JOEL

No!

Yasmin taps him again, and he turns.

YASMIN

You are known as Joel Smith?

                         JOEL

That's right.

                        YASMIN

I bring a message from the Hawk.

                         JOEL

The Hawk?

                        YASMIN

He said you would be searching for food.

She pulls a piece of paper out of her bodice and gives it to him.

                         JOEL

But...

Yasmin looks up at him, with some interest.

                        YASMIN

You will be joining him at the palace?

                         JOEL

Well, I...

                        YASMIN

We have much food there. Couscous.

She goes off, as Joel stares after her.

DISSOLVE

FULL SHOT - RECEPTION ROOM - DAY

The door bursts open and a harried Ahmed hurries in.

AHMED

A thousand pardons, sire, but...

CAID

Son of a cactus picker! What means this intrusion?

AHMED

I must speak to you–alone.

CAID

It had best be of the gravest importance.

(to Hiram)

Excuse me, my friend.

The two men move out of the room.

EXT. COURTYARD-DAY-FULL SHOT

The walled courtyard. It is beautifully tiled, and lined with exotic plants and shrubbery. In the center, conspicuous, is a well. Standing by the well is the DESERT HAWK, a fierce looking Arab, who wears a huge bull-whip on one side and a long Kumia sword on the other. Ahmed and the Caid move toward him.

CLOSER SHOT - AHMED, THE CAID, AND THE HAWK

CAID

(to Ahmed)

Who is this man?

HAWK

I am Sheik Hasim - The Desert Hawk!

                    CAID
                  (reacting)

What manner of lie is this?

                    AHMED

It is true, sire. Can there be any doubt?

                    CAID

Have you proof?

                    HAWK

If proof is needed.

He rolls back the sleeve of his burnoose and reveals his forearm.

CLOSE SHOT - FOREARM

Tattooed on the forearm is an easily recognizable hawk.

MED. SHOT - THE GROUP

The Caid is convinced.

                    CAID

We have blundered. The other man is an American!

                    HAWK

How could you have made such a stupid mistake?

                    CAID

He was mistaken for you because of the bird.

                    HAWK
                (almost to himself)

That bird is a grass-eater. I should not have trusted him with
such a delicate chore.

(to Caid)

How much does he know?

CAID

Everything.

HAWK

(drawing his sword)

I shall make him forget!

CAID

No. To kill an American so unjustly is to invite unnecessary trouble.

HAWK

(replacing his sword)

What do you suggest?

CAID

He must not know we suspect him. We will shower him with gifts.

HAWK

You are a bigger fool than I had imagined! This man must be disposed of.

CAID

(condescendingly)

I am not a child. Ahmed!!

                              AHMED

Yes, sire?

                               CAID

Fetch Tabout.

                              AHMED

                             (paling)

Tabout? The killer stallion?

                               CAID

                            (nodding)

Make haste. Tabout shall be my first gift to the American
pretender and my last!

                              AHMED

But sire, there is no way to bring Tabout. This week already
he has killed three grooms.

                               CAID

                            (vehement)

Grooms are dispensable! Bring the horse.

                              AHMED

Yes, sire.

Ahmed hurriedly leaves the SCENE, and the CAMERA MOVES IN
for a tighter SHOT of the Caid and the Hawk.

                               HAWK

You are a clever man. The horse will be a gift. He will never
suspect.

CAID

Exactly. We shall kill him with kindness!

The Caid and the Hawk exchange evil smiles as we.

FADE OUT

END OF ACT ONE

MIDDLE COMMERCIAL

ACT TWO

FADE IN:

EXT. PALACE-DAY (STOCK)-MED. SHOT

CUT TO:

EXT. PALACE GATE-DAY-MED. SHOT-JOEL AND GUARD

As Joel, attired in a flowing burnoose, approaches the gate. He stops, pulls a piece of paper from his pocket, reads it again to be sure he has understood Hiram correctly, then, satisfied, puts it away and moves past the guard with a confident air. Once safely in, he breathes a sigh of relief.

CUT TO:

EXT. COURTYARD-DAY-MED. SHOT - HIRAM AND THE CAID

As they enter the courtyard. Hiram is still carrying his umbrella, but he has left the falcon inside.

CLOSE SHOT - THE HAWK

Watching from a place of concealment.

MED. SHOT - HIRAM AND THE CAID

CAID

I have sent for Tabout, one of my finest Arabian horses.

HIRAM

Say, that sounds exciting.

CAID

It is a gift to the Desert Hawk.

HIRAM

(smiling)

Thank you.

CAID

(smiling)

We have heard you are a great equestrian.

CLOSE SHOT - HAWK

Smiling in anticipation.

MED. SHOT - HIRAM AND CAID

HIRAM

Of course, I've never tried. But I have formed some theories on equine psychology.

CAID

Of course.

HIRAM

It seems a simple matter of gaining the animal's confidence.

WIDER ANGLE

From o.s. come a few terrifying whinnies and snorts, and into the courtyard comes Ahmed, leading Tabout. He is indeed a beautiful white stallion, and from his eyes and nostrils come streaks of fire. He is rearing and lashing out with his hooves as a terrified Ahmed cowers back.

TWO SHOT - HIRAM AND CAID

As they observe the stallion.

CAID

That is Tabout.

HIRAM

Well now. It appears that my theory is about to be subjected to a most rigorous test.

CAID

He is impatient for his new master to ride him.

MED. SHOT - TABOUT

He is indeed impatient for something.

EXT. COURTYARD WALL – DAY - MED. SHOT - JOEL

As he moves to the gate, where he salutes another guard who opens the gate. Joel moves into the courtyard.

INT. COURTYARD – DAY - FULL SHOT - JOEL'S POV

As the horse jumps and rears, and Hiram begins to move toward it.

CLOSE SHOT - JOEL

As he closes his eyes in terror of what is about to take place.

FULL SHOT

As Hiram moves to a nearby bush upon which fruit of some sort is growing. He plucks off a piece of the fruit, as Ahmed lets go of the reins.

CLOSER SHOT - HIRAM

As he moves toward the horse, offering the fruit. He reaches the o.s. horse, who sniffs the fruit disdainfully, then belts it out of Hiram's hands with his nose and begins rearing anew.

(INTER CUT REACTIONS THROUGHOUT OF JOEL AND THE HAWK)

HIRAM

Hmm. It appears that he lacks the traditional sweet-tooth. I shall have to try alternate attack.

He begins to croon a little song. Hiram smiles, and speaks over his shoulder to the Caid.

HIRAM

(continuing)

I seem to have hit upon one of his favorites.

He continues to croon, finally reaching the horse, who is now gentled, and petting him on the nose.

TWO SHOT - AHMED AND CAID

Staring wide-eyed.

AHMED

It is impossible! He has killed a hundred men!

TWO SHOT - HIRAM AND HORSE

HIRAM

I suspect that was due to their inability to carry a tune.

Hiram is stroking Tabout's nose. Hiram taps Tabout behind the shoulder with his umbrella, and the horse drops to one knee, waiting for Hiram to mount him. Carrying his umbrella in the manner of a riding crop, Hiram vaults aboard and Tabout rises.

CLOSE SHOT - JOEL

He heaves a sigh of relief.

FULL SHOT

As Hiram, aboard the horse, puts him through a SERIES OF TRICKS. The horse rears, kneels, dances, etc., as we INTER CUT the reactions of the Hawk, Caid, Ahmed, and Joel.

MED. SHOT - AHMED, CAID

As the Hawk moves into the scene by their side.

HAWK

(watching Hiram o.s.)

This is no ordinary American. Let me deal with him my way.

Again he significantly touches the handle of his sword.

CAID

No! There is yet another way.

He extracts the plans from his burnoose, and hands them to the Hawk. He also removes the ring from his finger. The Hawk accepts this also.

CAID

(continuing)

Take the ring and the plans. Strike when you feel it is the proper time. I shall handle the American.

HAWK

If you should fail....

CAID

I shall not fail!

Nodding, the Hawk moves out of the SCENE.

CAID

(to Ahmed)

Come. Yasmin will know what to do.

AHMED

We dare not leave him alone. He will escape.

CAID

Through these walls? Never. The guard has been warned.

They move quickly from the courtyard.

FULL SHOT

Hiram and Tabout finishing the tricks. The horse bows, and Hiram looks around, seeing only Joel. He reacts to Joel in this strange guise.

JOEL

Hiram!

Hiram dismounts the horse and hurries to Joel.

MED. SHOT - HIRAM AND JOEL

> HIRAM

Hello, Joel.

> JOEL

What's going on here? That horse could have killed you!

> HIRAM

I believe that such was the intention.

> JOEL

Why? What did you do?

> HIRAM

The Caid apparently confused me with another gentleman... the Desert Hawk. He seems to have discovered his mistake.

> JOEL

But why didn't you tell me in your note?

> HIRAM

I was under close supervision. There is to be an attempt to blow up the fort, Joel, in which the Big Four are meeting.

> JOEL

There's no Big Four meeting here!

> HIRAM

I'm afraid there is.

> JOEL

Then we've got to get out of here!

HIRAM

My chances are microscopic. But I would advise you to depart through the same entrance through which you came, and report this situation to the authorities.

JOEL

What about you?

HIRAM

I'll manage, Joel. I have yet to capture Telea, you know.

Hiram, in the face of his danger, still manages to laugh it up a little. Joel, admiring his friend, grasps his hand.

JOEL

All right. Goodbye, Hiram, and good luck.

Joel moves out of the gate. As he does, Ahmed appears in the doorway.

AHMED

Sidi. The Caid requests your presence within.

Hiram surveys the walls for any method of escape, and seeing none, gives his characteristic shrug and moves off with Ahmed.

INT. PALACE - DAY-FULL SHOT

This is the same room as before. Now, however, it is apparent that the Caid is preparing to entertain. Two pretty native serving maids are spreading a sumptuous meal on a low table–bowls of skewered lamb, rice, couscous, fruits, sweet cakes, and jugs of minted tea. There are one or two native musicians present. The Caid is already seated behind the tables. The door opens and Ahmed ushers Hiram in.

MED. SHOT - THE CAID

As Hiram moves to the table.

CAID

Sit down, O Hawk. Your ride must have created an appetite.

HIRAM

This is most hospitable.

CAID

It is only the beginning. I have another gift for you.

The Caid CLAPS his hands.

FULL SHOT

The harem door opens, and two bare-torsoed guards enter the room, carrying a large, rolled up rug. They move to Hiram and the Caid, and deposit the rug in front of the table, unrolling it. As the rug opens, Yasmin, who has been rolled up inside, is revealed. She nimbly jumps from the rug, and bows to Hiram and the Caid.

CAID

You like my gift?

HIRAM

A beautiful offering. I shall have difficulty deciding in which room to use it.

The Caid and Yasmin exchange startled glances. Hiram bends down and feels a corner of the rug.

HIRAM

I'd judge it to be a rare Djebel Amour. Probably 15th century.

CAID

You have mistaken the wrapping for the gift! It is the girl -Yasmin.

HIRAM

How do you do?

YASMIN

I am yours to command, O Hawk.

HIRAM

This is awfully nice, but I am afraid I shall have to refuse.

CAID

You cannot refuse. She is the daughter of a king!

HIRAM

Are you sure her father would appreciate her association with a commoner?

CAID

The Hawk is no commoner. She will dance for you. The dance which will signal the beginning of your betrothal.

He claps his hands, as Hiram reacts, and the musicians begin an Arab song.

MED. SHOT - YASMIN

As she begins a sexy Arabian dance.

DISSOLVE:

INT. FORT – DAY - MED. SHOT - JOEL AND LT. BEAUCHAMPS

BEAUCHAMPS, attired in the uniform of the French Foreign Legion, is seated behind his desk, listening calmly to a harried Joel who is pacing back and forth.

JOEL

I'm telling you, lieutenant, they're going to blow up this fort! The most important men in the world are going to be murdered.

BEAUCHAMPS

(not believing it at all)

You're telling me, and your friend, Mr. - Mr.-

JOEL

Holliday. Hiram Holliday.

BEAUCHAMPS

Of course - Mr. Holliday - told you.

JOEL

That's right! They've got Hiram now. They're trying to kill him.

BEAUCHAMPS

Sometimes, Mr. Smith, the heat of the desert will do strange things to the mind of an otherwise rational man...

JOEL

How did I know there was a meeting?

BEAUCHAMPS

How indeed? Mr. Smith...the Caid's palace is out of my jurisdiction. Besides, every conceivable security precaution has been taken. There is no danger.

JOEL

All right. Have it your way. I'll go to the top.

He makes a move to leave.

BEAUCHAMPS

(sternly)

Mr. Smith! I suggest you stay, until I am able to check on you.

JOEL

What? How long will that take?

BEAUCHAMPS

We are quite thorough. Tomorrow, perhaps, or the next day.

JOEL

By then we'll all be dead!

Beauchamps only smiles at this mad American.

BEAUCHAMPS

Hardly.

CUT TO:

INT. PALACE – DAY - MED. SHOT - HIRAM, THE CAID, AND YASMIN

The meal is over. Yasmin is cuddled up to a distraught Hiram, as the Caid smiles. He looks at Yasmin, and gives her a signalling nod.

YASMIN

Would you come to the garden with Yasmin?

HIRAM

Well, I...

YASMIN

Please. We have much to discuss.

HIRAM

Oh really? I wasn't aware we had a common interest.

YASMIN

Our marriage.

HIRAM

(to Caid)

About blowing up the fort...

YASMIN

Come.

She takes his hand and literally drags him to his feet. The Caid's eyes meet Yasmin's as she turns while leading Hiram away. Their almost indiscernible nods tell the story. The Caid turns to Ahmed, who moves into the SCENE.

CAID

Follow them. You know your job.

Ahmed nods, and moves off.

EXT. COURTYARD-DAY - MED. SHOT

As Hiram and Yasmin enter the courtyard and move to the wall. Yasmin backs Hiram up against the well.

YASMIN

Why do you shy away from Yasmin? The very sight of you makes me shiver...

HIRAM

Perhaps a more substantial garment would alleviate the condition.

YASMIN

(backing off a bit)

Ah. You do not trust yourself with me. Is that not it?

HIRAM

That is not it.

YASMIN

(hurt shock)

You do not trust Yasmin?

HIRAM

Not entirely. If you'd excuse me...

He makes a move to go, but Yasmin pushes him back against the well again. She leans over and picks up a stone.

YASMIN

Perhaps Allah will smile and grant my wish...

She prepares to throw the stone into the well.

HIRAM

(turning and looking down into the well)

Is this a wishing well?

YASMIN

Yes.

HIRAM

Scientifically speaking, of course, that is merely a pleasant superstition.

He leans over and stares into the well.

MED. SHOT - AHMED

As he moves stealthily out into this courtyard.

MED. SHOT - HIRAM, YASMIN, AND AHMED

As Hiram is bent way over the well, Yasmin by his side. Yasmin turns and signals the approaching Ahmed.

HIRAM

Awfully deep, isn't it?

YASMIN

(meaningfully)

It is bottomless.

HIRAM

Oh, I doubt that. In order for any vessel to maintain....

As Ahmed has reached Hiram. He sets himself for the thrust, but Hiram turns just in time to realize the situation and move aside, sending Ahmed over the wall and into the well.

HIRAM

(to Yasmin)

Do you recall that I had previously stated that I did not entirely trust you?

YASMIN

Yes, but you do not think...

HIRAM

I wish to revise that statement. I do not trust you at all.

He turns, tips his hat, and starts out of the SCENE. Yasmin stops him.

YASMIN

Wait. You have won me over.

HIRAM

At this point I would consider that a rather hollow triumph.

YASMIN

Follow me.

She takes his hand and leads an unwilling Hiram toward a door which opens into the courtyard. She opens the door.

YASMIN

Go. You will be safe in here.

She pushes Hiram in, then slams the door shut and locks the bolt. She smiles triumphantly, then hurries out of the SCENE.

INT. HAREM – DAY - FULL SHOT

There are five or six lovely girls in the room. They react to Hiram's entrance, and scream. Hiram reacts, tries the door, and finds it locked.

HIRAM

Say. This is distressing.

CUT TO:

INT. PALACE – DAY - MED. SHOT - YASMIN

As she runs into the room and confronts the Caid.

TWO SHOT - YASMIN AND THE CAID

CAID

It is over?

YASMIN

He got away!

CAID

What?

YASMIN

But he will not get far. He is in the harem.

CAID

He has entered the harem? For this he shall die at my hands.

He rises and picks off a fierce-looking sword from the wall. He moves toward the harem door, as the rest of the people in the room (servants, a guard or two, Ahmed) watch in wide-eyed silence. He reaches the harem door. It opens before he touches it, and four or five scantily clad harem girls exit, led by a guard.

CLOSER ANGLE - GIRLS

As they file past CAMERA. The girl at the end is sadly miscast. It is obviously Hiram, trying to sneak out. He has thrown a harem outfit over his suit, and the veil doesn't even begin to cover his glasses. The tip of his umbrella is visible under the garment's hem.

CLOSE SHOT - CAID

As he observes Hiram, and smiles evilly.

MED. SHOT

As Hiram moves by the Caid, the Caid rips away the veil. He brandishes the sword menacingly.

CAID

Prepare to die, American infidel!

Hiram jumps back.

HIRAM

I believe I shall have to refuse.

Furious, the Caid dives after Hiram, swinging the sword viciously. Having no other protection, Hiram parries the blow with his umbrella.

ANOTHER ANGLE

As Hiram and the Caid duel across the room. The tide of battle is fluctuation as the combatants duel out the door toward the courtyard. Yasmin and the remainder of the people follow them out.

EXT. COURTYARD – DAY - FULL SHOT

As Hiram and the Caid enter, duelling. For a moment they come together as their weapons lock.

TWO SHOT - HIRAM AND CAID

HIRAM
(smiling happily)

Say. This is exhilarating!

WIDER ANGLE

As they break apart and continue the duel. A few more passes and they come together again.

TWO SHOT

CAID

You are possessed by the devil himself.

HIRAM
(beaming)

Thank you.

WIDER ANGLE

As they break apart. Hiram and the Caid are now fencing dangerously close to the well. Hiram stumbles against the well and it appears for a moment that he might fall in, but he recovers his balance just as the Caid, spotting an advantage, lunges at Hiram. Hiram ducks and at the same time his umbrella flies open, plummeting the Caid over the rim of the well and down.

CLOSE SHOT - HIRAM

As he stands by the well, looking down. Long moments pass and there comes no sound from the well. Hiram's face wrinkles in a puzzled frown, when there comes the faint SOUND of a splash. Hiram relaxes, and salutes into the well.

HIRAM

I guess we have exploded the theory of the bottomless well.

ANOTHER ANGLE

To include Hiram, Yasmin, and the girls. A couple of guards come running into the scene. Hiram runs off quickly, threatening them with a deadly umbrella.

DISSOLVE:

INT. FORT – DAY - MED. SHOT - BEAUCHAMPS AND JOEL

Joel is seated, smoking nervously, as Beauchamps, ignoring him, is working at his desk.

JOEL

How long is this going to take?

BEAUCHAMPS

Patience, Mr. Smith.

JOEL

Patience! Hiram might be dead and we're sitting in the middle of a booby-trap about to blow sky high. How can I be patient?

Beauchamps smiles, and goes back to work. The door to the office opens and another soldier enters and salutes.

BEAUCHAMPS

Yes?

OFFICER

Sheik Hasim is here, sir. On the parade grounds.

BEAUCHAMPS

Very good.

The soldier exits, and Beauchamps rises.

BEAUCHAMPS

Would you like to come along, Mr. Smith? Perhaps Sheik Hasim is your Desert Hawk and you will be permitted a choice view of the explosion.

He laughs uproariously at the improbability of it all and ushers a disconsolate Joel out of the room.

EXT. FORT PARADE GROUND – DAY - MED. SHOT - THE HAWK AND HENCHMAN

As he waits. He is now accompanied by a henchman, also wearing a whip. The HENCHMAN removes his whip and begins to flick it aimlessly at the ground, snapping at rocks and bits of debris.

HAWK

(low)

Our timing must be perfect.

He glances down and fondles the ring on his finger.

HENCHMAN

When you throw the ring–will we not be destroyed with the fort?

HAWK

It is a chance we are well paid to take.

WIDER ANGLE

As Beauchamps and Joel reach the Hawk and his henchman.

> BEAUCHAMPS

Welcome, Sheik Hasim.

CUT TO:

EXT. FORT – DAY - MED. SHOT

A uniformed guard is standing by the gate. Suddenly he reacts.

ANOTHER ANGLE

Revealing Hiram, hurrying toward the gate of the fort. Still attired in the Harem garment and carrying the falcon on his wrist, he is a ludicrous sight indeed. He walks right by the guard.

> HIRAM

Excuse me.

As Hiram enters the fort, the guard suddenly regains his composure.

> GUARD

Stop! Come back here!

He moves off after Hiram.

CUT TO:

EXT. PARADE GROUNDS – DAY - MED. SHOT - BEAUCHAMPS, JOEL, HAWK, AND HENCHMAN

> BEAUCHAMPS

They are there, Sheik Hasim. A mere stone's throw away.

He points, o.s.

MED. CLOSE SHOT - A BUILDING (STOCK)

The Group's POV.

MED. SHOT - GROUP

> BEAUCHAMPS

The greatest minds in all the world are discussing your problem. Your people have nothing to fear.

CLOSE TWO SHOT - HAWK AND HENCHMAN

As they exchange meaningful glances. He stares again at the ammo deposit.

> HAWK

You are right. They are but a stone's throw.

The CAMERA PANS DOWN as he slowly removes the ring. Suddenly, from o.s., comes the VOICE of the guard shouting "stop."

MED. SHOT - GROUP

As they react.

MED. SHOT - HIRAM

Hurrying toward him, the guard hot on his heels.

MED. SHOT - GROUP

> JOEL
> (happily)

Hiram!

> HAWK

It is him! The American!

Hiram joins the group, a bit out of breath and deadly serious. The guard quickly comes into the scene and jams his rifle into Hiram's back.

BEAUCHAMPS

What is the meaning of this?

HIRAM

I really don't think there's time to explain.

He indicates Hasim.

HIRAM

(continuing)

This man's the Desert Hawk. I think you'll find he intends to blow up the fort.

BEAUCHAMPS

You're mad.

HAWK

No. He is right. But it is too late.

Deliberately, he slips the ring from his finger and hurls it in the direction of the ammo dump. Quick as a flash, Hiram uncaps the falcon, circles his arm, and releases the bird.

HIRAM

Sha-hou!

MED. SHOT - THE RING

As it sails through the sky.

MED. SHOT - THE GROUP

As they react.

JOEL

He...he caught it!

Hasim is frightened now, Beauchamps unbelieving, and Joel relieved. Hasim's henchman has dropped to the ground and is cowering there. Hiram remains stone-faced as the bird alights on his wrist. Hiram takes the ring from his beak and hands it to Beauchamps.

HIRAM

I would suggest you have it disarmed at once.

Beauchamps stares at the ring.

HAWK

You have foiled me, American, but you shall never take me alive.

He breaks away, but Hiram, noticing the henchman's whip lying on the ground, quickly picks it up and lashes it out at the fleeing Hasim. The whip curls around his legs and brings him to the ground as the guard, having recovered his composure, rushes up and leads the Hawk away.

BEAUCHAMPS

Mr. Holliday, is there any way we can reward you?

CLOSE SHOT - HIRAM

Ridiculous in the Harem outfit.

HIRAM

Yes. Do you happen to have a spare burnoose?

FADE OUT

FINAL COMMERCIAL

FADE IN:

FULL SHOT - MOROCCAN CAFÉ - DAY

Joel is seated eating as Hiram enters.

> HIRAM

Good morning, Joel.

> JOEL

Nothing good about it, Hiram. Look.

He hands some paper over to Hiram, as Hiram sits down.

> JOEL

> (continuing)

Just got my story back from military censorship. "Top Secret." Can't print a word.

> HIRAM

Well, we all have our little problems.

> JOEL

"We all have our little problems???" What problems have you got like this?

He indicates his story.

> HIRAM

While it may not seem important to you, Joel...

He breaks off and looks around, as the girls from the harem come in, led by Yasmin. They take up a position behind Hiram at the table. Joel stares.

JOEL

Hiram! You mean...since you disposed of the Caid...that you...you...?

HIRAM

Certainly not, Joel. I'm merely chaperoning them to America...they're entered in the international tournament of beauty.

JOEL

Oh.

(slight pause)

Then what's your problem?

HIRAM

Telea Sphingdae. I find that the spotted hawk-moth has been extinct in these parts for some years. To think of the time I've wasted here.

JOEL

Wasted?

He looks at Hiram, to the harm girls, then back to Hiram again.

FADE OUT

THE END

The Adventure of the Vanishing House

This was the nineteenth script to be commissioned and the seventeenth episode to air. NBC ran it on 23 Jan 1957 whilst the BBC showed it on 25 December 1960 and again on 26 July the following year. The script was written by Richard M Powell.

FADE IN:

ESTABLISHING SHOTS – PARIS – DAY - (STOCK)

The distinctive Paris landmarks are seen.

DISSOLVE THRU TO:

EXT. SHOP-DAY-FULL SHOT

JOEL and HIRAM come into the picture in front of a small pastry shop. Joel stops, inhaling deeply.

> JOEL

Smell that air, Hiram. The heady wine of Paris.

> HIRAM

I have a slight head cold, Joel.

He takes out his inhaler for a slight drag.

> JOEL

It's not a head cold, Hiram... you have no romance in your soul! Can't you sense the restless ghost of Francois Villon... the rustle of the gown of Madame Pompadour...the marching feet of Napoleon's Grand Army?

Hiram thinks it over, then shrugs. Joel looks at him.

> JOEL

> (continuing)

No romance in your soul at all. I'm going to get some éclairs.

He goes into the pastry shop. As Joel leaves the scene, a GIRL runs breathlessly up to Hiram. She is French, young, pretty, and seems badly frightened.

ROXANNE

Monsieur! Monsieur! It is my father...I cannot find a gendarme...They will kill him!!!

HIRAM

Really?

ROXANNE

There is no time...they have followed him here from our
own country...What am I to do, Monsieur??

HIRAM

I suggest that you guide me to the scene.

ROXANNE

Alone, unarmed...you would come with me??

HIRAM

Why not?

ROXANNE

Then come...quickly!

She takes his arm and leads him quickly off. Joel appears at the door
of the pastry shop, looking after Hiram. He gives a puzzled shrug
and then goes back inside.

QUICK DISSOLVE TO:

EXT. HOUSE - FULL SHOT

Roxanne comes in quickly, leading Hiram, and goes to the door of
the small house.

ROXANNE

In here! Quickly!

HIRAM

Excuse me.

He steps through the door ahead of her. Roxanne follows.

REVERSE SHOT - AT DOOR

Roxanne cries out, staring.

ROXANNE

Father!!!!!

P.O.V SHOT

A MAN is bound to a chair in the center of the room. He is gagged and is looking toward Hiram and Roxanne with an expression of terror. A large, TICKING bomb, wired to a clock, is beside the chair.

WIDER ANGLE

Hiram and the girl start toward the man in the chair. Hiram sees something and stops the girl.

HIRAM

One moment.

ROXANNE

But the bomb...it is about to go off!

HIRAM

I know. But the approach would appear to be booby-trapped.

ROXANNE

I....I do not understand.

Hiram gingerly lifts the rug in front of the chair.

INSERT - FLOOR

There are some large land mines on the floor.

BACK TO SCENE

HIRAM

Land mines. It would seem they were quite thorough.

ROXANNE

They are friends! You must hurry!

HIRAM

There is a saying in my country that haste sometimes makes waste.

He makes a path by shoving the mines aside with the tip of his umbrella and goes to the chair to examine the bomb.

CLOSER SHOT - AT CHAIR

Hiram looks at the clock.

HIRAM

(to the girl)

Do you have the time?

She takes a quick glance at her wristwatch.

ROXANNE

It is one-fifteen. But....

HIRAM

I believe I have forty-five seconds.

The man shakes his head violently. The girl interprets for him.

ROXANNE

My father says leave him! You will die!

HIRAM

Not unless my nail clippers fail me completely.

He has his nail clippers out and is preparing to go to work on the bomb. The girl whirls and cries out a warning.

ROXANNE

Look out!!

Hiram rises quickly to face the danger.

FULL SHOT

Two ASSASSINS, with masks over their eyes, are advancing on Hiram. One carries a rapier, the other a pistol. Hiram raises the umbrella to give battle to the rapier, manoeuvring so that the man with the pistol cannot get a clear shot at him. In the ensuing battle, INTER CUT with reactions of Roxanne and the man in the chair. Hiram is hopping among the land mines to avoid stepping on them and trying to fight off his two opponents so that he can get back to the bomb. He has his nail clippers in one hand and makes several passes at the bomb wiring as he flies by but to no avail. Hiram at one point disarms the man with the gun by hitting his hand with the umbrella, but the man goes after the gun with the other hand, and is just about to shoot when Hiram whirls and puts his umbrella tip in the gun barrel. He then manages to disarm the man with the rapier, and gets to the bomb just in time to prevent it from going off.

CLOSER SHOT - AT CHAIR

Hiram straightens up.

HIRAM

There, I believe that covers everything.

ROXANNE

You were magnificent!

HIRAM

Really? Thank you. If you'll hold my umbrella. I'll untie your father.

CERVEAU

(taking off the gag)

That will not be necessary, thank you.

He rises from the chair, casting off the ropes. Hiram stares. Cerveau is a large man, of dignified mien, and an Oxford accent.

HIRAM

Say, that's a pretty good trick.

CERVEAU

I have many. As have you. Bandage these incompetents, Roxanne.

He gestures to the two assassins.

HIRAM

I gather that this was not exactly the real thing.

CERVEAU

A test. I have heard of you, Hiram Holliday. I had to see for myself. You will do.

HIRAM

Thank you. Do what?

Before answering, Cerveau goes to a cabinet, takes out a brandy bottle, and pours a glass for Hiram and one for himself.

TWO SHOT - HIRAM AND CERVEAU

Cerveau gives Hiram a glass.

CERVEAU

I am called Le Cerveau...translated, The Brain. My associates and I have a small operation under way here. We are tunnelling into the vault of The Bank of France...it adjoins the rear of this building.

HIRAM

That's very industrious of you.

CERVEAU

It is nothing. A means to an end. The few millions we shall obtain there...merely working capital.

HIRAM

I see.

CERVEAU

The money will open the doors to more money...and pay more eyes not to see and mouths not to speak. My course is already started. In six months I shall be the master of France, in a year more the ruler of the Continent or quite dead.

HIRAM

(ambiguously)

Well, here's hoping you make it.

They clink glasses.

CERVEAU

I shall.

He drains his glass, then hurls it to the floor.

HIRAM

If that's all, I'd best be going.

He puts his glass down and turns to go.

CERVEAU

One moment. I need men, Hiram Holliday. Men, their kind I can always get.

He gestures in the direction of the vanquished assassins.

HIRAM

If I hear of anybody, I'll let you know.

CERVEAU

I did not stage this little charade for amusement, my dear sir. You are the man I must have above all others.

HIRAM

Thank you, but I'm already employed.

CERVEAU

What will you have? Money? A woman?

Roxanne comes into the picture.

CERVEAU

(continuing)

A country, then.

HIRAM

I must decline, in spite of the fact that I should like very much to own Holland. I'm quite fond of tulips.

CERVEAU

Decline today. You will accept tomorrow.

HIRAM

I think not and of course you realize I'll have to report this to the police. Tunnelling into the Bank of France, that is.

CERVEAU

Of course, by all means.

ROXANNE

Cerveau!

CERVEAU

A man of honor could do no less.

HIRAM

I'm glad you see my side of it. Well, goodbye for the present.

CERVEAU

Au 'voir.

Hiram starts to go, pushing a few mines with his umbrella. He then looks more closely at the tip.

HIRAM

Say, I believe that was a real bullet in the gun.

CERVEAU

Of course. Had you not been able to avoid it, I would not have needed you.

HIRAM

Oh.

He goes and Roxanne turns furiously on Cerveau.

ROXANNE

Why did you let him go?? Fool! Fool!! He will bring the gendarmes!!

CERVEAU

Let him. When they come, we shall be ready.

ROXANNE

But why do you take such a chance??

CERVEAU

Because, Roxanne, I must have this Hiram Holliday. You understand? I must have this man.

QUICK DISSOLVE TO:

EXT. SHOP - FULL SHOT

Joel is emerging from the shop with a bag of éclairs. He is sampling one as Hiram comes up to him.

JOEL

Where have you been, Hiram? I thought I saw you chasing a girl.

HIRAM

I was not chasing her, Joel. She commandeered me to save her father.

JOEL

Sure.

HIRAM

Really. Actually, he was not in physical peril.

JOEL

(nodding)

Um-hm.

HIRAM

I don't think he was even her father.

JOEL

Well, this is Paris, Hiram.

HIRAM

What he was really doing was tunnelling into the Bank of France.

This is too much even for Joel.

                    JOEL

Now, wait a minute...

                    HIRAM

That's why I have to notify the authorities.

                    (calls)

Gendarme!

                    JOEL

Hiram.

                    HIRAM

Yes, Joel?

                    JOEL

Nothing. Nothing.

A GENDARME comes up. He is smiling, polite, and anxious to help the two obvious Americans.

                  GENDARME

Oui, Monsieur?

                    HIRAM

How do you do? I suppose I wish to report a crime.

                  GENDARME

A crime, Monsieur?

HIRAM

Yes, down the street. Some men are digging a tunnel into the Bank of France.

The gendarme takes another look at Hiram. He then breaks into a smile.

GENDARME

I see, an American joke.

He laughs and Hiram joins in politely, then breaks off.

HIRAM

Not really, no.

GENDARME

No?

HIRAM

No, I think we'd better hurry.

The gendarme restrains him.

GENDARME

A moment, Monsieur. How did you find out about these... these tunnel diggers?

HIRAM

They told me.

GENDARME

They told you?? Your friend also?

                    HIRAM

No, he was buying éclairs.

The gendarme looks at Joel, who answers rather helplessly.

                     JOEL

I was buying éclairs.

                    HIRAM

It's really quite simple. You see...

                  GENDARME

Excuse.

He leans in to sniff Hiram's breath. He straightens up, satisfied.

                  GENDARME

                 (continuing)

Ah, I see.

                    HIRAM

You mean the brandy? I just took a sip of that when he asked
me to join the gang.

The gendarme is now sure of the situation, and speaks more tolerantly.

                  GENDARME

The head excavator.

                    HIRAM

Yes, after I rescued him by defusing the bomb.

GENDARME

(nodding)

The bomb.

HIRAM

Actually, I told my friend here all about it. He saw the girl lead me off.

Joel wants to help.

JOEL

Yes.

The gendarme turns to him.

GENDARME

You also saw the chief digger?

JOEL

No, but he was the girl's father.

HIRAM

Not really her father, Joel.

GENDARME

Her grandmama?

HIRAM

It's very simple. You see, after I disarmed the two assassins...

JOEL & GENDARME

(together)

Two assassins???

HIRAM

(to Joel)

I forgot to tell you. Except they weren't really assassins.

JOEL

I think we'd better go back to the hotel, Hiram.

HIRAM

But we can't, Joel! I have to show the gendarme where they're tunnelling into the bank vault!

The gendarme takes charge, talking hold of Hiram's arm.

GENDARME

Of course, but first we arrest the Groundhog Gang, who tunnel into the bank, and then back to the hotel, for the well-earned sleep. No?

HIRAM

Yes, you see, Joel?...I told you it was all very simple.

Hiram and the gendarme start off and Joel, with a confused bite on his éclair, follows.

QUICK DISSOLVE TO:

EXT. STREET – DAY - FULL SHOT

Hiram, the Gendarme, and Joel walk into the picture. Hiram is leading, talking over his shoulder to the other two.

HIRAM

This is the place. It was right past that tobacco stand. Right here.

He turns and reacts.

P.O.V. SHOT

In place of the house formerly occupying the spot, there is nothing but a Punch and Judy show, being watched by several children.

ANOTHER ANGLE

GENDARME

Well, Monsieur?

HIRAM

Say, this is strange.

GENDARME

Why? Behold!...the Groundhog Gang!

JOEL

Hiram...

HIRAM

I'm sure this is the place, Joel.

GENDARME

Of course! Why do you not say...Gendarme! Arrest these puppets!

HIRAM

I find this most curious. Not ten minutes ago there was a house here.

Joel, for the first time in their association, is losing faith.

JOEL

I think we'd better go, Hiram.

GENDARME

Do that Messieurs and I will undertake the dangerous capture.

He indicates the puppets. Hiram looks at them, and then looks more closely.

HIRAM

Say, this is strange.

JOEL

Why?

HIRAM

Look at Punch, Joel.

JOEL

What about him?

HIRAM

He looks exactly like Le Cerveau...the head of the gang.

GENDARME

Indeed?

All three crowd in for a closer look.

CLOSE SHOT - PUPPET STAGE

The face of Punch does indeed bear a close resemblance to Le Cerveau. He carries a shovel, and is endeavouring to entice Judy within swatting range.

PUNCH
(sweetly)

Judy! Judy!

He takes a swipe, misses, and cackles with frustration.

CLOSE SHOT - HIRAM, JOEL, AND GENDARME

HIRAM

Yes, the resemblance is undeniable.

The other two look at him, while he looks at the puppets.

GENDARME

Really?

HIRAM

Say, Judy closely resembles the girl. His daughter, only she wasn't his daughter. Look.

The other two keep looking at Hiram, who keeps staring at Judy.

JOEL

Hiram...

HIRAM

You saw her, Joel.

JOEL

I only saw her back.

ANOTHER ANGLE

The watchers and the puppets are both visible. Hiram addresses Judy.

HIRAM

Would you turn around, please?

Punch reaches out with his shovel and bops Hiram on the head, screaming with rage. Hiram jumps back.

CLOSE SHOT - PUPPET STAGE

PUNCH

(to Judy)

Ah, this is what goes on. You flirt with a strange man.

He is hopping up and down in rage.

JUDY

Monsieur Punch. Strange, yes, but I do not flirt with him.

PUNCH

You flirt with him. While I work away in a hot tunnel, all for
a few million from the bank vault.

He takes another swipe at her with his shovel.

ANOTHER ANGLE

Joel and the Gendarme exchange a look. Together, they draw Hiram
a short distance from the puppets.

HIRAM

Well, I guess that proves my story. He admitted he was tunnelling into the bank vault.

GENDARME

Monsieur Punch?

HIRAM

He's only disguised as Punch.

GENDARME

Disguised?

HIRAM

Actually, it's Le Cerveau...The Brain. The head of the gang.

GENDARME

I thought his disguise was quite good.

HIRAM

Well, it's not really a disguise. It's...

JOEL

Hiram, we understand.

HIRAM

(happily)

You do, really?

GENDARME

Of course, Monsieur. You have not been drinking.

HIRAM

Hardly.

GENDARME

It is far more serious.

HIRAM

Indeed it is. They might be getting close to the bank vault.

GENDARME

It is far more serious in here.

He touches Hiram's head with his finger.

> HIRAM

Joel, tell him how ridiculous that is.

> (beat)

Joel?

> JOEL

He'll be all right, officer. He just needs rest.

> HIRAM

Joel!

> GENDARME

A long rest. He is in your charge, Monsieur.

He turns to the puppets.

WIDER ANGLE

> GENDARME

Adieu, Mamselle Judy....

> (tips his cap)

Adieu, Monsieur Punch.

Punch reaches out and whacks him with his shovel, then cackles in delight, as the Gendarme jumps back.

> GENDARME

> (continuing; recovering, to Hiram and Joel)

A most dangerous man. Good day, Messieurs.

He goes off.

TWO SHOT - HIRAM AND JOEL

Hiram is looking after the Gendarme.

> HIRAM

Joel, he didn't believe my story.

> JOEL

We'd better go, Hiram.

> HIRAM

You don't believe it either?

> JOEL

We'll talk about it back at the hotel.

> HIRAM

Gladly, after I warn the Bank of France.

> JOEL

What??

> HIRAM

You stay here and keep an eye on the gang, Joel.

He indicates the puppets.

> JOEL

Hiram, I couldn't persuade you not to warn the bank?

> HIRAM

Hardly, I have nineteen hundred francs on deposit there...
five dollars and forty-three cents. Be back in a minute, Joel.

WIDER ANGLE

He goes off, as Joel stares after him.

MED. SHOT - BEHIND STAGE

Le Cerveau and Roxanne are crouched behind the stage. They lower their puppets, as Cerveau looks through a peek hole in the stage. He is manipulating Punch, while Roxanne holds Judy.

CERVEAU

Ah, he goes.

ROXANNE

Why must we do all this, Cerveau?

CERVEAU

I have told you...I must have this man. When I have broken him down and when he has realized his own great resources cannot cope with mine. Then, Hiram Holliday will belong to us.

Roxanne takes a look through the peek hole.

ROXANNE

His friend...he approaches.

MED. SHOT - FRONT OF STAGE

Joel is wandering over, curiously. He gets to the now empty stage and starts to put his head through to see over it. Punch suddenly erupts, swatting Joel with his shovel and cackling madly. Joel jumps back.

CLOSE SHOT - JOEL

He is rubbing his head, totally mystified.

FADE OUT

MIDDLE COMMERCIAL

FADE IN:

EXT. BANK OF FRANCE - DAY-FULL SHOT - (STOCK)

If possible, this is the Bank of France. If not available, almost any imposing building.

DISSOLVE THRU TO:

INT. OFFICE - FULL SHOT

Hiram is being ushered into the office of an officer of the bank by a uniformed bank guard. From behind his desk, MONSIEUR DUFEAUX rises to greet the visitor.

DUFEAUX

Bonjour, Monsieur.

HIRAM

Bon jour. Je m'appelle Hiram Holliday. Je suis un deposant ici.

DUFEAUX

Ah, you are a depositor here. You will sit down, Monsieur Holliday?

CLOSER ANGLE - AT DESK

HIRAM

Thanks, but I really don't have time. I just come to warn you.

DUFEAUX

Warn me?

                    HIRAM

Yes, about your vault. A gang is digging a tunnel into it.

                    DUFEAUX

A gang? Digging??

                    HIRAM

Yes, have you heard any strange noises recently?

                    DUFEAUX

No.

                    (pointedly)

Have you, Monsieur?

                    HIRAM

I suggest that we listen a moment.

                    DUFEAUX

                    (doubtfully)

Oui.

They listen. There is a DULL EXPLOSION, off. All react.

                    HIRAM

I believe they're using dynamite.

                    DUFEAUX

Monsieur Holliday. They blast for a new subway tunnel.

                    (to the guard)

They do blast for a subway tunnel?

The guard nods and Dufeaux is reassured. He continues, to Hiram.

DUFEAUX

(continuing)

Your deposit is quite safe, Monsieur.

HIRAM

Nineteen hundred francs. Five dollars and forty-three cents.

DUFEAUX

Then I appreciate your great concern. Stop in at any time, Monsieur.

HIRAM

I hate to make a nuisance of myself, but I'd feel much better if you looked for yourself. On the other side of the block.

DUFEAUX

Of course, but the Paris police are most efficient.

HIRAM

I told a gendarme. He didn't seem to believe me.

DUFEAUX

Encroyable

HIRAM

But that was because the gang had changed into puppets.

DUFEAUX

Diabolique.

HIRAM

They want me to join them.

DUFEAUX

You would fit in quite well.

HIRAM

(continuing)

Nooo....I do not believe so. A rather puritan conscience would prevent me from enjoying ill-gotten gains.

Dufeaux takes Hiram's arm, to lead him to the door.

FULL SHOT - OFFICE

DUFEAUX

Monsieur Holliday, go home and rest well. I personally shall guarantee the safety of your five dollars and forty-three cents.

HIRAM

That's most generous of you.

There is another EXPLOSION, louder and nearer. Dufeaux reacts, as does the guard.

HIRAM

(continuing)

But they're getting closer.

DUFEAUX

It is the subway tunnel, I am certain. Almost certain. Puppets?

HIRAM

My friend is keeping an eye on them. Around the block.

There is another EXPLOSION.

DUFEAUX
(a bit shaken)

I believe the walk shall do us both good.

(to the guard)

Come.

All three go toward the door.

QUICK DISSOLVE TO:

EXT. STREET-DAY - FULL SHOT

Hiram, Dufeaux, and the guard walk into the picture. Hiram is leading, talking over his shoulder to the other two.

HIRAM

Although it appears to be a harmless Punch and Judy show, in reality...

He stops and turns.

P.O.V. SHOT

The puppet stage is gone and has been replaced by the original small house.

CLOSE SHOT - HIRAM

He reacts.

HIRAM

Well now.

DUFEAUX

The little men...You have lost them?

HIRAM

Yes, but I can explain rather easily.

DUFEAUX

Of course.

HIRAM

You see, the first time I was here, the house was here.

DUFEAUX

I see.

HIRAM

That's when the head of the gang was bound to a chair, with a time bomb ready to go off.

DUFEAUX

Time bomb?

HIRAM

Not really, but we can skip that.

DUFEAUX

I am most grateful.

HIRAM

Then, when I came back with the gendarme, the house was gone, and instead there was a puppet stage.

DUFEAUX

Why not?

HIRAM

It seems quite apparent that they are attempting to discredit me.

DUFEAUX

They shall never succeed.

HIRAM

Thank you. Shall we go in?

DUFEAUX

Of course. Après vous.

Hiram goes to the door. Dufeaux exchanges a look with the guard and follows.

CLOSE SHOT - AT DOOR

Hiram pauses at the door.

HIRAM

I believe that under the circumstances, I shall enter without knocking.

He opens the door and goes in. After another exchange of looks with the guard, Dufeaux follows.

INT. ROOM - FULL SHOT

As Le Cerveau rises from a chair, Roxanne runs to Hiram and throws herself upon him, showering him with kisses.

ROXANNE

Hiram, you have returned, my darling! You have come back
to Roxanne.

TWO SHOT - DUFEAUX AND GUARD

They react in some astonishment.

FULL SHOT - ROOM

Hiram tries to disengage, turning to Dufeaux.

HIRAM

I trust that you are not deceived by this subterfuge.

ROXANNE

Hiram, you are still strange? But I do not care you have come
back.

She again covers him with kisses, pushing him back into a chair and
sitting on his lap. Le Cerveau comes closer to Dufeaux.

CERVEAU

You are a friend of the...afflicted?

DUFEAUX

No, a director of the Bank of France, Monsieur. Arsene
Dufeaux.

CERVEAU

Monsieur Dufeaux. I am a psychiatrist...he has been under
my care for some time.

Hiram tries to object.

HIRAM

But...

ROXANNE

Darling!

She silences him with kisses. Cerveau turns back to Dufeaux.

CERVEAU

He should perhaps be committed...but it would break the girl's heart. She is mad for him.

DUFEAUX

I see.

(hesitates, then delicately)

Might I inquire why?

CERVEAU

(shrugs)

A mystery.

HIRAM

But...

ROXANNE

Hush, bel ami.

She kisses him again.

CERVEAU

(turns back again)

He spoke to you of the puppets?

DUFEAUX

They were digging a tunnel into the bank.

CERVEAU

Ah, he suffers from severe Lilliputianism.

DUFEAUX

Je ne comprends pas.

CERVEAU

He seeks to reduce the adult world in size, so that he does not feel afraid of the "big" people. A rare form of infantilism.

HIRAM

I...

ROXANNE

I do not care, my beautiful Hiram. Roxanne does not care.

She again kisses him.

DUFEAUX

He is...harmless?

CERVEAU

Quite. I thank you for bringing him home.

DUFEAUX

Not at all.

(to Hiram)

Adieu, Monsieur Holliday.

HIRAM

But...

He is again silenced by Roxanne. Dufeaux and the guard go out.

REVERSE SHOT - OUTSIDE DOOR

Dufeaux pauses, with a slight sigh.

DUFEAUX

A most fortunate madman.

INT. ROOM - FULL SHOT

Cerveau waits at the door to make sure Dufeaux and the guard are gone, then turns to Roxanne.

CERVEAU

They are gone, Roxanne.

She is involved in her work. Cerveau speaks more sharply.

CERVEAU

(continuing)

Roxanne! They are gone.

She rises reluctantly. Hiram also gets up.

CERVEAU

(continuing to Hiram)

You are sorry that I drove your friends away?

HIRAM

Not entirely, no.

He arranges his hair.

                    CERVEAU

You now see the futility of holding out against me, yes?

                     HIRAM

Not completely. Although you are quite resourceful.

                    CERVEAU

Thank you. We shall make a formidable team.

                     HIRAM

There seems no way of convincing you of my essential honesty.

                    CERVEAU

Honesty is a matter of law. You and I together...we shall make
our own laws.

                     HIRAM

If you'll excuse me, I must hunt up my friend, Joel Smith.

                    ROXANNE

Why not look here?

                     HIRAM

You mean you've kidnapped him?

                    CERVEAU

I am most resourceful.

                     HIRAM

Then you leave me no choice.

                    CERVEAU

You are joining us.

HIRAM

I am going for the authorities. Good day.

CERVEAU

Au revoir

He smiles as Hiram goes out the door.

ROXANNE

Again you let him go!

CERVEAU

The hunter, Roxanne, knows that the tiring fox runs in a circle. Once more around–

(he makes a circling gesture)

–and he will be mine.

QUICK DISSOLVE TO:

EXT. STREET – DAY - FULL SHOT

This is the section of street in front of the bakery shop. Hiram appears, calling to a gendarme who has his back to Hiram.

HIRAM

Gendarme! Gendarme!

The gendarme turns as Hiram comes up to him. There is the shock of mutual recognition.

TWO SHOT - HIRAM AND GENDARME

GENDARME

You called "Gendarme?"

HIRAM

Nothing personal, but I was rather hoping it would be a different gendarme.

GENDARME

Monsieur. I have been most patient.

(suddenly)

Back, to the hotel.

HIRAM

I shall have to refuse. You see, my friend Joel Smith has been kidnapped.

GENDARME

Ah, the little puppets?

HIRAM

In a way. Except that they aren't puppets any more. They've put back the house.

GENDARME

The house?

HIRAM

Yes, where I saved the girl's father from...

(breaks off)

Never mind. It's right down here. You'll come?

GENDARME

No, no, no, no, no!

                        HIRAM

Then I suppose I'll have to get someone else.

                      GENDARME

You are not leaving my sight.

                        HIRAM

Really?

                      GENDARME

Without a doubt.

                        HIRAM

Good. Let's go.

He turns and runs off in the direction he indicated. The startled Gendarme reacts, then gives chase.

QUICK DISSOLVE TO:

EXT. STREET – DAY - FULL SHOT

Hiram pulls up to a stop, looking back as the panting Gendarme catches up.

                        HIRAM

You see? Here's the house.

He turns, then reacts.

P.O.V SHOT

The puppet show is back. Punch is again trying to lure Judy within swatting range.

                        PUNCH

Judy! Judy!

TWO SHOT - HIRAM AND GENDARME

> HIRAM

I wonder how they do that?

> GENDARME

Monsieur...come along.

> HIRAM

But, I can't leave Joel here.

> GENDARME

So? Which one is Joel?

CLOSE SHOT - PUPPET STAGE

Punch takes a swipe at Judy, with much cackling. She screams for the police.

> JUDY

Gendarme! Gendarme!

A puppet enters in an old-fashioned, formal policeman's outfit, with a three-corner Napoleon hat. The face bears a strong resemblance to Joel.

TWO SHOT - HIRAM AND GENDARME

Hiram reacts.

> HIRAM

It's Joel! You remember Joel.

The Gendarme stares, then stares at Hiram.

> GENDARME

But he has shrunk, Monsieur.

HIRAM

That proves they have him. I demand formal action.

GENDARME

Of course. But what?

HIRAM

I have not time to look up the appropriate statute. The matter is urgent.

GENDARME

Yes, at midnight, they all turn into pumpkins.

HIRAM

But...

He turns. A lively fight is developing among the puppets.

CLOSE SHOT - PUPPET STAGE

Punch, Judy, and the policeman are engaged in a noisy brawl. Hiram and the Gendarme edge closer and are swatted by the puppets. Both jump back.

GENDARME

You will remain here, Monsieur. I will summon the wagon.

HIRAM

For me?

GENDARME

Not for them.

He gestures at the puppets. Hiram looks, then reacts.

CLOSE SHOT - PUPPET STAGE

A figure with the face of Hiram timidly makes an appearance.

TWO SHOT - HIRAM AND GENDARME

> HIRAM

Look!

The Gendarme looks.

ANOTHER ANGLE

The Hiram puppet vanishes.

> HIRAM

You may find this hard to believe, but I saw a puppet bearing a strong resemblance to myself.

> GENDARME

I summon the wagon...now.

He starts off and the Hiram puppet makes another appearance.

> HIRAM

Look!

The Gendarme whirls around, as the puppet vanishes.

> GENDARME

Yes?

> HIRAM

Nothing, I suppose you had better summon the wagon.

> GENDARME

Oui!

He goes off. Hiram approaches the stage.

CLOSE SHOT - AT STAGE

Hiram approaches, the other puppets clear the stage and the Hiram puppet appears.

> HIRAM
>
> (to puppet)

How do you do?

> PUPPET
>
> (with Hiram's voice)

Hello, stupid.

Hiram reacts slightly and Cerveau raises his head above the stage level, putting the puppet down.

> HIRAM

You are quite accomplished.

> CERVEAU

Thank you. You see the futility of further resistance?

> HIRAM

At the moment, yes.

> CERVEAU

Excellent judgment. Just step this way, please.

He indicates that Hiram should come around the stage.

> QUICK DISSOLVE TO:

INT. TUNNEL - FULL SHOT

There is a ladder resting against the side of a tunnel apparently blasted out of solid rock. Cerveau climbs into view down the ladder, followed by Hiram. Cerveau carries a cane.

> CERVEAU

Look around, Mr. Holliday.

> HIRAM

> (looking)

Quite roomy, isn't it?

> CERVEAU

Blasted out of solid rock. The people at the bank will be most astonished.

> HIRAM

Hello, Joel.

ANOTHER ANGLE

Joel lies bound and gagged, against a wall of the tunnel.

> CERVEAU

I do not believe we can use him. It is too bad.

> HIRAM

Well, c'est la vie.

CLOSE SHOT - JOEL

He reacts at Hiram's betrayal.

FULL SHOT - TUNNEL

CERVEAU

Come forward. Perhaps you can give my crew some pointers on the proper use of dynamite.

HIRAM

Gladly. Goodbye, Joel.

CLOSE SHOT - JOEL

Joel's staring eyes watch Hiram out of sight.

FULL SHOT - TUNNEL

The two men who attacked Hiram previously are working at the end of the tunnel, placing some dynamite sticks in prepared holes in the rock. Hiram and Cerveau come into the scene.

CERVEAU

Gentlemen...may I present a new member of our organization?

HIRAM

How do you do?

The men straighten up and one of them speaks.

MAN

A great blade. Welcome, Monsieur.

HIRAM

Thank you. May I?

He takes one of the dynamite sticks and inspects it closely. He then sniffs it.

CERVEAU

Is anything wrong?

> HIRAM

A rather high percentage of kieselguhr. Could I have a match, please?

> MAN

A match?

> CERVEAU

Give it to him.

He hands the match to Hiram.

> HIRAM

Thank you.

He strikes it on the wall of the cave, then holds it under the stick of dynamite.

> MAN

Look out! What do you do?

> HIRAM

Dynamite is not particularly sensitive, unless heated. At 350 degrees Fahrenheit, however, a mere breath will send it off.

> CERVEAU

How...how hot is a match?

> HIRAM

I don't believe I know.

He blows out the match and tests the temperature of the stick.

HIRAM

(continuing)

Oooh.

CERVEAU

Put it down!

Hiram takes up a fencing attitude, with his umbrella in one hand and the dynamite in the other.

HIRAM

Gentleman, I think you had better yield.

MAN

He has tricked us!

HIRAM

I am afraid so.

CERVEAU

Fools! He will not destroy himself. Attack!

The men grab up digging tools and go after Hiram. He parries the swing of one with his umbrella, and holds up the stick of dynamite in the path of a pick axe swung by the other man. The man desperately stops his swing in mid-air.

MAN

He would kill us all!

The two men scramble past Hiram and towards the entrance to the tunnel.

> HIRAM

I shall have to round them up at a later date.

> CERVEAU

I do not think so.

> HIRAM

Really?

> CERVEAU

Like you, Hiram Holliday, I have studied in secret. For many years. Together, we could have owned the world. Now, I must bring my own deadly skill into play.

He draws his sword cane.

> CERVEAU

> (continuing; lunging)

Die!

Hiram leaps aside from the lunge and the duel is on. It rages up and down the tunnel, with Hiram managing to cheat death by parrying with his umbrella and threatening Cerveau with the dynamite in the other hand. They duel to where Joel lies bound, and he watches with his eyes in INTERCUT CLOSE SHOTS. The two antagonists lock.

TWO SHOT - HIRAM AND CERVEAU

> CERVEAU

Do you think I fear the dynamite? I choose complete victory...or sudden death!

HIRAM

Say, do you mind if I don't join you?

FULL SHOT - TUNNEL

They spring apart. Hiram gains a little ground as he presses the attack and Cerveau almost goes down. Hiram puts the stick of dynamite gently in Joel's lap.

HIRAM

Would you hold this, Joel? It slows me down.

Joel reacts in horror. The duel continues, and Hiram finally disarms his opponent, who bares his breast.

CERVEAU

Strike! To be vanquished by an umbrella...grant me the boon of the coup de grace!

HIRAM

I couldn't, really. But, I won't say anything if you tell the police it was a rapier.

Hiram quickly removes Joel's gag.

JOEL

Hiram! Get this dynamite away from me!

HIRAM

It isn't really that sensitive, Joel. It was a subterfuge.

He takes the stick and throws it down the tunnel. There is a loud EXPLOSION and a fall of rocks. Hiram, Joel, and Cerveau all duck, then slowly raise their heads again.

JOEL

Hiram! What did you do??

Hiram peers down the tunnel, through the dust.

HIRAM

I believe, Joel, that I've broken into the Bank of Paris.

FADE OUT

FINAL COMMERCIAL

FADE IN:

EXT. STREET – DAY – FULL SHOT

Hiram and Joel are standing together, beside the puppet stage. The Gendarme approaches them.

GENDARME

Bonjour, Monsieur Holliday.

HIRAM

Bonjour, mon capitaine.

GENDARME

Bonjour, Monsieur Smith.

JOEL

Bonjour, bonjour.

ANOTHER ANGLE

The Gendarme passes the puppet stage, where the figures of Hiram and Joel in their puppet identities are on stage. The Gendarme nods to them.

GENDARME

Bonjour, Monsieur Holliday...Monsieur Smith.

He takes another step or two, then pauses.

CLOSE SHOT - GENDARME

What he has just seen sinks in, and baffles him completely. He thinks, then gives up and goes on, with a Gallic shrug.

FADE OUT

Ingram Content Group UK Ltd.
Milton Keynes UK
UKHW020621260423
420802UK00010B/372